Intimacy
with God

Intimacy with God

Thomas Keating

CROSSROAD · NEW YORK

1994

The Crossroad Publishing Company
370 Lexington Avenue, New York, NY 10017

Copyright © 1994 by St. Benedict's Monastery, Snowmass, Colorado

Chapter 13, "The Charismatic Renewal and Contemplation," is re-
printed, with the permission of Paulist Press, from *Contemplation and
the Charismatic Renewal*, edited by Paul Hinnebusch, OP (Paulist Press,
1986).

For information on any events or programs of Contemplative Outreach, contact the National Office of Contemplative Outreach Ltd.,
9 William St., Butler, NJ 07405. Tel: 201-838-3384.

Printed in the United States of America

Library of Congress Cataloging-in-Publication Data

Keating, Thomas.
    Intimacy with God / Thomas Keating.
        p.   cm.
    Includes bibliographical references.
    ISBN 0-8245-1390-8
        1. Contemplation.   2. Mystical union.   3. Spiritual life–Catholic
    Church.   4. Catholic Church–Doctrines.   I. Title.
    BV5091.C7K4185   1994
    248.3'4–dc20   93-37790
                                                                CIP

Contents

———————————

6 / Contents

Acknowledgments

THE MATERIAL FOR THIS BOOK began as a series of talks given over a number of years and to a wide variety of audiences, ranging from advanced practitioners of Centering Prayer to those completely unfamiliar with it. My thanks to the staff and participants of the Centering Prayer retreats and workshops who first heard these talks and gave useful feedback.

Assembling a book from such a variety of sources requires considerable editorial effort, and again I have had the good fortune to rely on the teamwork of Bonnie Shimizu, Cynthia Bourgeault, and Patricia Johnson. Bonnie worked closely with me in the initial selection, arrangement, and editing of material as well as in the transcription of many of these chapters from their original format as informal (sometimes impromptu) talks. Developmental editor Cynthia Bourgeault gave the material its final form and helped me clarify a number of important points. The devoted secretarial services of Patricia Johnson allowed the manuscript to arrive at the publishers on schedule.

And finally I must thank the monastic community of St. Benedict's, Snowmass, and especially its abbot, Fr. Joseph Boyle, who have supported this work in every aspect, from the simple logistical tasks of printing and duplication, to the extraordinary commitment to the building of a new retreat center to better accommodate the contemplative reawakening and the ongoing work of Contemplative Outreach. The new buildings are underway even as the final words are being put on this manuscript, giving concrete substance to the vision that the Christian contemplative tradition is no longer limited just to the cloister, but to all those who seek God in the depths of their hearts.

Snowmass
November 1993

Prologue

G OD IS PRESENT TO EVERYTHING like the eye of a camera that sees everything just as it is. Yet we, in our
turn, may not be present to God. Like the subjects of a casual photograph, we may not perceive that someone sees a
marvelous value and beauty in us and is taking our picture.

We are summoned into the presence of God by the fact
of our birth, but we become present to God only by our
consent. As our faculties and capacities to relate gradually
develop and unfold, the capacity to enter into relationship
with God increases, and each new depth of presence requires a new consent. Each new awakening to God changes
our relationship to ourselves and to everyone and everything else. Growth in faith is growth in the right perception
of all reality.

In the beginning, the light of faith may resemble the
rays of the sun filtering through a stained-glass window
and illuminating the various tints and delicate intricacies
of the glass, along with its cracks and flaws. Thus the light
of faith filters through our human faculties, manifesting,
along with the evidence of human frailty, the beauty and
goodness of our personhood.

A higher intensity of faith resembles the rays of the
sun pouring through a transparent window, an experience
of light that is much more powerful. At times, the glass
seems to be transformed into light. Similarly, surrender to
the light of faith leads to a more intimate relationship with
God — even to a kind of identification that deepens the
experience of the divine presence, giving it a wholly new
meaning and perspective.

There is a further possibility. Suppose that the window-
pane is shattered, leaving in place of the glass a great open

9

hole. The light would then no longer be a relationship but an experience of oneness. Divine love, the ripe fruit of faith, gradually changes the perception of ordinary reality into insight and the divine presence into oneness.

Is it the function of those who are ardently seeking God to linger at the moments of insights, or simply to let reality speak for itself and, like the lens of a camera, to open ourselves to the light?

Chapter 1

The Origins of Centering Prayer

CENTERING PRAYER IS A METHOD of prayer that comes out of the Christian tradition, principally *The Cloud of Unknowing*, by an anonymous fourteenth-century author, and St. John of the Cross. It brings us into the presence of God and thus fosters the contemplative attitudes of listening and receptivity. It is not contemplation in the strict sense, which in Catholic tradition has always been regarded as a pure gift of the Spirit, but rather it is a *preparation* for contemplation by reducing the obstacles caused by the hyperactivity of our minds and of our lives.

The historical roots of Centering Prayer reach back to St. Joseph's Abbey in Spencer, Massachusetts, where I was abbot from 1961 to 1981. This was during the time of the first wave of the renewal of religious life after the Second Vatican Council, when many questions were raised for the first time and interreligious dialogue was encouraged by the Holy See. Several of us at Spencer became acquainted with groups from other spiritual traditions who resided in our area. We invited several spiritual teachers from the Eastern religions as well as some ecumenically skilled Catholic theologians to visit and speak with us. Fr. Thomas Merton was still alive at this time and writing extensively about his researches and exchanges in interreligious dialogue. He was one of the most articulate pioneers from the Christian side in the dialogue among the world religions.

In a similar spirit we entertained a Zen master who wished to visit our monastery. We invited him to speak to the community and later to give a sesshin (a week-long intensive retreat). For nine years after that, he held sesshins once or twice a year at a nearby retreat house. During those years I had the privilege of making several sesshins with him. On the occasion of his first sesshin held in our monastery, he put on the Cistercian habit and ate with us in the refectory. We have a picture of him on his seventieth birthday eating a piece of cake while sitting in the half lotus posture.

We also were exposed to the Hindu tradition through Transcendental Meditation. Paul Marechal, a former monk of Holy Cross Abbey in Berryville, Virginia, a daughter monastery of Spencer, had become a TM teacher and offered to instruct us in the practice. Many in the community wanted to experience it.

Exposure to these traditions, as well as conversations with visitors to our monastery who had benefited from them, naturally raised many questions in my mind as I tried to harmonize the wisdom of the East with the contemplative tradition of Christianity that I had been studying and trying to practice for thirty years.

The basic meditative practice of Benedictine and Cistercian monks is Lectio Divina, a way of reading the Scripture with a deepening prayerful attentiveness that moves toward contemplation. I had noticed over the years that the practice itself had become obscured because of the plethora of reading material now available under the general heading of Lectio Divina. The original practice had expanded from the attentive reading of Scripture or commentaries by the early Fathers of the Church to include spiritual reading in the broadest sense of the word. In the process, the emphasis had shifted from deepening one's prayer to intellectual stimulation. Meanwhile, prayer itself had become so rigidly dichotomized — discursive meditation, affective prayer, and the multiplication of devout aspirations — that the inherent tendency of Lectio Divina to move toward contemplation had been lost. Contemplation was regarded as an exceptional gift, not as the normal flowering of Lectio Divina and Christian prayer.

I was aware that the method of Lectio Divina in most

instances was not doing the job of bringing people, even cloistered monks and nuns, to the contemplative states of prayer that St. Teresa describes in her writings: infused recollection, the prayer of quiet, the prayer of union, and the prayer of full union. All are deepening experiences of the presence of God.

I had entered the monastery to become a contemplative. I chose the hardest order I could find because in those days austerity of life was believed to be the necessary means of reaching contemplation. The Trappists were a good choice for such a project. They had a long tradition of penitential exercises that goes back to the monastic reform of LaTrappe in the seventeenth century. The reform was at least partially influenced by Jansenism, the very negative view of human nature and the body eventually condemned by the Holy See. Silence was the rule of the monastery; indeed, novices normally spoke only to the abbot and novice master for the first three years. There was little opportunity for conversation beyond those brief interviews. During those early years I had not the remotest idea of the history and the aspirations of the other monks. I didn't even know their family names.

Why were the young disciples of Eastern gurus, Zen roshis, and teachers of TM, who were coming to the abbey in the 1970s for dialogue, experiencing significant spiritual experiences without having gone through the penitential exercises that the Trappist order required? These young people manifested a great appreciation for the values of silence, solitude, and fidelity to a regular meditative practice. It was inspiring to meet young people who were putting in twenty to thirty minutes of meditation twice a day in spite of being in college or professional life, while active religious, priests, and cloistered monks and nuns seemed to have a hard time putting in a half hour of mental prayer a day.

I also became aware of the deep contemporary hunger for spirituality. In the wave of spiritual reawakening that the Second Vatican Council seems to have touched off, young people were going to India by the thousands from all over the world in search of spiritual teachers. Some spent several years there under horrendous physical conditions. They adapted to poverty, exposure, sickness, and bad food in order to satisfy their hunger for an authentic spiritual path.

My thought was, well, this is fine. I was not knocking the seriousness of Zen practice or denying that many people were benefiting from it as well as from other Eastern practices. But why were thousands of young people going to India every summer to find some form of spirituality when contemplative monasteries of men and women were plentiful right here in this country? This raised the further question, Why don't they come to visit us? Some did, but very few. What often impressed me in my conversations with those who did come was that they had never heard that there was such a thing as Christian spirituality. They had not heard about it in their parishes or Catholic schools if they had attended one. Consequently, it did not occur to them to look for a Christian form of contemplative prayer or to visit Catholic monasteries. When they heard that these existed, they were surprised, impressed, and somewhat curious.

Our monastery at Spencer served as a drawing card for some of them living in the New England area. They liked to come and talk about their practices and experiences. Many were having experiences very similar to what Christian tradition calls contemplation. Although I had studied the Christian tradition deeply and had tried to practice it, I had found that when I talked about it in conferences to the monastic community, many of the monks would be turned off. They didn't want to hear about contemplation. The priests who came to the guest house for retreats did not want to hear about it either. They had been trained in the seminary to think that contemplation belonged in cloisters and had no relation to what they were doing. If parish priests and professors in Catholic seminaries did not feel that contemplation was suitable for them or for their students, naturally lay folks did not either.

Not only was there a negative attitude toward contemplation prior to about 1975, but the word "contemplation" itself had become so ambiguous that the popular mind identified it with a lifestyle rather than with a form of prayer. The term was generally limited to mean a special kind of lifestyle requiring an enormous amount of renunciation that the average person could not possibly envisage, either because one had no attraction or vocation for it, or because one's duties in the world made it impossible.

Sometime in the mid-1970s, I raised the following question in a conference to our monastic community: "Could we put the Christian tradition into a form that would be accessible to people in the active ministry today and to young people who have been instructed in an Eastern technique and might be inspired to return to their Christian roots if they knew there was something similar in the Christian tradition?" Having devoted my life to the pursuit of the Christian contemplative tradition and having developed a profound appreciation of its immense value, I grieved to see it completely ignored by people who were going to the East for what could be found right at home, if only it were properly presented.

When I raised this challenge to the community, Fr. William Meninger was inspired to take it seriously. Basing himself on a fourteenth-century spiritual classic, *The Cloud of Unknowing*, he put together a method that he called the "Prayer of the Cloud" and started teaching it to priests in the retreat house. The response was so positive that he decided to put his conferences on audio tapes. Those tapes have sold over fifteen thousand copies and have been a take-off point for many people to use the simple form of prayer recommended by the author of *The Cloud of Unknowing*, in which a single word such as "God" or "Love" expresses one's "naked intent direct to God."

About this time our community was asked by the Religious Committee of the Major Superiors of Men of the United States to help them with their prayer. By the early 1970s the intense social activism that had dominated the previous decade had lost some of its fascination. After the Second Vatican Council many priests and religious had rushed into ghettos without being adequately prepared for the burdens of such a ministry. They burned out, ending up in some cases doing less in the service of others than they would have if they had stayed where they were. With the best of intentions they had taken on ministries that required a depth of inner resources they just did not have.

Major superiors of religious orders were also experiencing the wear and tear of the profound upheavals in religious life following the Second Vatican Council. The committee approached Fr. Basil Pennington, another monk of Spencer, who was well known to the Religious Conference of Men through meetings he attended on canon law, for some practical assistance. We asked ourselves how and in what form we might present the method of prayer based on *The Cloud of Unknowing* that Fr. William Meninger was teaching to priests in the guest house.

Fr. Basil gave the first retreat to a group of provincials, both men and women, of various religious congregations at a large retreat house in Connecticut. It was they who suggested the term "Centering Prayer" to describe the practice. The term may have come from their reading of Thomas Merton, who had used this term in his writings.

Beginning in 1976, Fr. Basil started teaching Centering Prayer in the form of introductory workshops in Spencer's guest house, first to priests and then to other people who wanted to come. After a couple of years, we realized that we could not accommodate all the people who wanted to attend and set about devising an advanced workshop that we hoped would enable the participants to become teachers of this method so that it could be offered elsewhere. The advanced workshop called for a session of four periods of prayer of twenty minutes each with a five-to-ten minute silent walk between the periods. Some people in the community, as well as visitors coming to the guest house, complained that it was spooky seeing people walking around the guesthouse like "zombies." When I resigned as abbot in the fall of 1981, Spencer dropped the workshops and went back to the former nondirective style of retreat.

I headed for St. Benedict's Monastery, our foundation in Snowmass, Colorado, with no intention of teaching Centering Prayer. But in May 1982, I was asked by the assistant pastor in Aspen to offer a presentation on prayer once a week for four consecutive weeks. A small mention of the event was put in the parish bulletin and, to our surprise, about eighty people showed up. After that, I gave several retreats in Trappist and Benedictine monasteries, in which I gradually developed the material for the Spiritual Journey video tape series, which was filmed in the late fall of 1986.

In the summer of 1982 I paid a visit to the Lama Foundation in New Mexico, an ecumenical community of spiritual seekers. Ram Dass happened to be there giving a workshop at the time, and I spoke to the group at his invitation. At least half of them were Catholics and a significant percentage were Jews; the rest were a sprinkling of other aligned and nonaligned persons. I was struck by these numbers and wondered, "Where are these Catholics coming from?" Many of them were disaffected from the religion of their youth because of the legalistic and overmoralistic teaching that many had received in their local parishes and Catholic schools; they now felt spiritually enriched by their experiences in Buddhism and Hinduism.

At Lama they were pleased with my respect for Eastern religions, as most of them had not previously met a priest who was sympathetic with their experience. Catholics also found me sympathetic to the problems they had encountered with their early upbringing. During the first couple of years in my new home in Colorado, I visited several Eastern communities, where I continued to find the same

Negative
from

percentages of Catholics. The bitterness and indignation of these former Catholics was often directed at me as a priest, so much so that I felt a little like a garbage man on a collecting expedition. At the time, clearly, the Church was not projecting an image of spirituality, at least not in a way that ordinary persons could perceive it.

Lama invited me to offer a program at its Intensive Studies Center in August 1983, and I accepted. For some time I had wanted to put together a Christian contemplative retreat that would be comparable to a Zen sesshin, with a significant amount of time spent in silent meditation, an experiment that had not been done before in the Christian tradition as far as I was aware. It is true that three or four hours of meditation are prescribed in the Spiritual Exercises of St. Ignatius on an enclosed thirty-day retreat, but it is highly programmed with regard to the subjects on which one is to reflect and the visualizations one is to use. I was curious to learn what effect long periods of non-programmed prayer every day for two weeks might have on ordinary Catholics.

It turned out to be a watershed experience. I chose a two-week retreat because I thought it might take twice as long for us to do what is done in a Zen sesshin in a week. I also did not want to overwhelm the participants, so we did only five hours of contemplative prayer each day. I also presented the material that later appeared on the Spiritual Journey video tapes, with an introduction to Lectio Divina and, of course, instruction in the practice of Centering Prayer. Silence was observed throughout the day, and time for discussion was provided in the evenings.

This retreat took place under very primitive conditions. The shock effect of no hot water, no indoor plumbing, no electric lights, and no phone unless one hiked half a mile drew the twelve participants out of their usual routines, to say the least, and bonded them tightly together. Half of the participants at that original Lama retreat are now pillars of the Contemplative Outreach network. They include

Gail Fitzpatrick-Hopler, Fr. Carl Arico, Fr. Bill Sheehan, and Mary Mrozowski, who later, with David Frenette, founded Chrysalis House, a contemplative live-in lay community in Warwick, New York. Pat Johnson and Mary Ann Matheson were members of the Lama Community at the time, serving the workshops given there at the Foundation. They now staff the monthly Intensive Workshops at the monastery in Snowmass. The experience at Lama convinced me that the Christian contemplative tradition was alive and well and could be communicated in a workshop with dramatic effects for the grounding of a personal contemplative practice.

In November 1983, Gus Reininger, while on retreat at St. Benedict's, broached with me the idea of forming an organization that would teach Centering Prayer in parishes. As an experiment, I agreed to conduct a parish workshop that Gus and his wife Gale quickly organized for December 1983 at St. Ignatius Loyola Church in New York City. Subsequent workshops followed that spring and summer conducted by myself, Fr. Basil Pennington, and Fr. Carl Arico. Over 175 parishioners attended these events, and thanks to this warm response and the support of the pastor, the late Victor Yanitelli, S.J., our instinct that Centering Prayer had a place in parish life was verified.

Meanwhile, Ed Bednar, working at the Thomas Merton Center at Columbia University under the direction of Columbia chaplain Rev. Paul Dinter, expressed to me his interest in forming a network of contemplatives. This seemed a good complement to the unfolding experiment centered at St. Ignatius. Ed and Gus had exploratory meetings with a number of religious figures from the metropolitan New York area — Fr. David Toolan, S.J., Fr. James Lopresti, S.J., Br. David Stendal-Rast, O.S.B., Fr. Daniel Berrigan, S.J., Fr. Paul Dinter, Fr. Carl Arico, and others. The shared enthusiasm generated by these meetings resulted in an organization we christened Contemplative Outreach. Our goals, ambitious at that time, were to offer Centering Prayer in parish and diocesan contexts, to train facilitators and teachers, and to develop materials. Thanks to the support of Cardinal John O'Connor and Bishop Joseph O'Keefe, we were able to secure two foundation grants to fund a pilot program for the archdiocese of New York. Contemplative Outreach's first Centering Prayer event was a workshop at Holy Trinity Church attended by more than 350 persons, from which sprung additional workshops and support groups in a number of other parishes. Along with this effort we coordinated already existing support groups, founded by Mary Mrozowski, in New Jersey and Long Island. Contemplative Outreach was underway.

A small group, constituting a board for Contemplative Outreach, began meeting regularly at the Merton Center to coordinate the various support activities, adopt a mission statement, and chart a course for the future. First Ed Bednar and then Mary Mrozowski served as temporary executive directors. Gail Fitzpatrick-Hopler became our first full-time executive director.

In the original vision statement of Contemplative Outreach we identified ourselves as "a network of faith communities committed to the process and transmission of Christian transformation." In service of that vision and the thousands of people who are dedicated to Christian contemplation, Contemplative Outreach now sponsors workshops and retreats that encourage extensive formation in the Christian journey and the experience of Centering Prayer. In addition to the ten-day Intensive Retreats, Advanced and Post-Intensive Retreats have been developed to deepen the process.

A Formation for Contemplative Outreach Service Workshop is held several times a year to provide for intensive study of the essentials of Centering Prayer and the Christian journey, and Contemplative Issues Workshops provide opportunities to discuss questions that arise as people's experience of the journey unfolds. Our vision statement concludes with the affirmation, "It is Christ who empowers us to live the contemplative dimension of the Gospel in everyday life." It is this affirmation that has allowed us to evolve to where we are now, and it is the place out of which all new growth will come.

Chapter 2

Attitudes toward God

THE CHRISTIAN SPIRITUAL PATH is based on a deepening trust in God. It is trust that first allows us to take that initial leap in the dark, to encounter God at deeper levels of ourselves. And it is trust that guides the intimate refashioning of our being, the transformation of our pain, woundedness, and unconscious motivation into the person that God intended us to be.

Because trust is so important, our spiritual journey may be blocked if we carry negative attitudes toward God from early childhood. If we are afraid of God or see God as an angry father-figure, a suspicious policeman, or a harsh judge, it will be hard to develop enthusiasm, or even an interest, in the journey.

These negative images of God, which are implanted in us largely as a result of early religious training, are in fact a legacy of past generations and a pervasive set of religious attitudes that represent a distortion — sometimes a 180-degree distortion — of scriptural and gospel values. This is true for both Protestants and Catholics, although its imprint has been felt particularly vividly in the Catholic Church.

Prior to the Second Vatican Council (1962–66), a syndrome of attitudes about God that has been labeled the "Western Model of Spirituality" was generally communicated in catechism classes and religious instruction. The term is used by Fr. Richard Hauser, S.J., a professor at Creighton University, in his book *In His Spirit*. "Spirituality" should be put in quotation marks because the understanding of God that was communicated did not faithfully represent the teaching of Scripture; rather, it showed the heavy influence of the eighteenth-century Age of Reason, with its thought processes dominated by the philosophical dualism of René Descartes and its worldview shaped by Newtonian physics, with the grand image of God "out there," managing a mechanical universe from a majestic distance. The bottom line, according to Fr. Hauser, was a rigidly dualistic sense of "self-outside-of-God," and "God-outside-of-self." This dualism might be characterized by the conviction that down here on earth, completely separated from God, we search, suffer, and struggle, while from some distant heaven God watches and judges.

According to Fr. Hauser, many college students continued to reflect these dispositions even after the Second Vatican Council. These tend to be unconscious but strongly held attitudes that arise spontaneously unless they have been evaluated and updated by a mature judgment. You may recognize some of them by recalling your own early religious instruction.

The first attitude that flows from the Western Model of Spirituality is that external acts are more important than internal acts. The term "external acts" refers to rituals or to the exercise of good works such as fasting, almsgiving, and bodily penances. The term "internal acts" refers to the motives out of which these acts emerge. The former can come from pride and self-centeredness as easily as from love of God and respect for others. Jesus' teaching in the gospels is clear: "Clean the inside of the cup first and then worry about the outside."

The second attitude that flows from the Western Model of Spirituality is that the self initiates all good works and God rewards them. When articulated theologically, this belief comes close to the Pelagian heresy. It brings to mind the image of battling in an arena to placate God for one's sins or to win God's favor, while God sits passively in the bleachers watching the contest. If we do well, it is thumbs up; if we fail, it is thumbs down. The gospel, on the contrary, teaches that God initiates all good deeds through the inspiration of the Spirit abiding within us, while we listen attentively and put into action what the Spirit suggests.

The third attitude that flows from the Western Model of Spirituality is an overarching concern about getting to heaven rather than exercising the love of God and neighbor here and now, as strongly emphasized in the preaching of Jesus. This concern was sometimes expressed by efforts to accumulate merits in this life in order to require God, so to speak, to reward us in the next. Following is a caricature of the "good" Catholic gentleman prior to the Second Vatican Council as perceived by the Western Model. He attends Sunday mass faithfully, never eats meat on Friday, contributes generously to the collection every Sunday. He goes to confession and Communion at least once a year and expects that on his death bed a priest will be there with the Last Rites to anoint him so that he can at least get to purgatory and then after a brief detainment, shortened by means of masses offered for the repose of his soul, move on to heaven to be amply rewarded for his exemplary Catholic life. It might never have occurred to this man that it might be a sin to exasperate or dominate his wife, to shout at the children, to underpay his servants and employees, or to disregard the poor just down the street or in his parish. In short, he adheres to the dogmas and observes the externals of the Catholic religion but fails to practice the gospel. The gospel is a life to be lived, not just a set of observances.

This caricature is not too far-fetched. Before the Second Vatican Council there was a climate that favored bargaining with God, so to speak, to avoid hell or to shorten purgatory. So-called meritorious deeds were exaggerated out of all proportion, an attitude accompanied by a naive disregard for what Scripture clearly states regarding the good we are able to do in and of ourselves. For example, the gospel urges us to love God here and now and to love our neighbor with the same unconditional love with which Jesus has loved us. Excessive concern about future rewards or punishment tended to take ordinary people's attention away from their primary duty of manifesting here and now the love of Christ toward their neighbors. This emphasis on future reward led the Christian people to underestimate the duty of social action, a responsibility that in recent centuries was largely left to religious orders to fulfill.

Human nature prefers to offer substitute sacrifices to placate God rather than to offer the sacrifice that God clearly states in Scripture is the only acceptable one, which is the gift of ourselves. Underlying much external religious practice lies the terror of a god who condemns to hell and the need to placate him. This is the attitude of Typhonic consciousness, the level of consciousness proper to primitive peoples and to children from ages two to four. There is a certain magical approach in this kind of observance: "If I faithfully attend mass every Sunday and confess my sins, even though I never change the value system that is causing them, everything will be okay."

The Scriptural Model of Spirituality, rediscovered by Christian scholars and emphatically endorsed by the documents of the Second Vatican Council, enabled the Church to recognize, recapture, and start to renew Christian teaching and values from the pure source of Scripture. Through the scholarly study of the original meaning of words and the cultural context in which Scripture was written, we probably have a better understanding of the actual intent of the scriptural authors in our time than any generation since the death of the apostles.

The Scriptural Model represents a 180-degree turn from the Western Model. Scripture teaches that interior motivation is more important than external acts. As Jesus said to the Pharisees, "The Sabbath was made for people, not people for the Sabbath." The Pharisees in his day were following traditions made by human beings, not the Law of Moses and the inspired tradition of the prophets.

Tradition is not the same as traditions. Christian tradition is the *living experience* of the gospel. Its practice demolishes the false self system, with its false values and

excessive demands based on our wounded sense of who
we are and our consequent need to compensate. One *lives*
tradition. One expresses it in one's life and in one's reactions to life as a genuine response to Jesus Christ. *Traditions*
are human interpretations and are often exalted above the
love of God and neighbor. Jesus inveighed against such
attitudes. He said to the Pharisees, "You lay impossible burdens on people's backs and do nothing to lift them. You do
not enter the kingdom yourselves and you prevent others
from doing so." The Pharisees were good moralists and
could make good distinctions, but the motives for their
religious observance, at least according to the four Evan-
gelists, were overlaid by vanity and pride. They went to
great lengths to gain attention, even to the extent of sound-
ing trumpets to announce when they were giving alms.
Jesus excoriated the hypocrisy of the Pharisees while show-
ing profound compassion for prostitutes and for the tax
collectors, who were the chief extortioners of the time.

It is not the Western Model's self-outside-of-God that
initiates works that are truly inspired by God, but the
self-in-God and God-in-the-self. In the Scriptural Model of
Spirituality the Spirit dwells in us as the dynamic source of
inspiration for all our good deeds, and we consent. The emphasis in the New Testament is on listening and responding
to the Spirit rather than initiating projects that God is expected to back up, even though God had little or nothing to
do with them.

Once the starting point of the spiritual life was separated from faith in the Divine Indwelling, people began to
conceive of God "out there." If God is "out there," especially in some distant heaven, how is one going to climb up
to God? If we fall on our faces after a few steps, as is normally the case, we may conclude, "I guess this is not for me.
God and I do not seem to get on." It is impossible to pass
through the trials of the spiritual life if we think that God is
a million miles away and that we have to climb up to God,
or that we have to make ourselves worthy of God.

The Scriptural Model of Spirituality emphasizes developing union with God here and now and working in the service of those in need. In fairness to the Western Model, we have to say that there was a certain abstract recognition of the importance of the Holy Spirit, but it was well hidden in ordinary catechetical instruction. In my youth the Holy Spirit used to be called the "forgotten guest." That is like forgetting the person you have been married to for fifty years and, as the family celebrates your fiftieth anniversary, wondering what this strange person is doing in your house.

This neglect of the presence and action of the Holy Spirit in our lives did not facilitate the spiritual journey. We were more likely to conclude, "I'll leave the journey to cloistered monks and nuns." And the corollary was, "Write them a letter and have them pray for me." Then we could feel free to do our own thing as long as we subscribed to the Creed and fulfilled the required ritual obligations. We were misinformed. A good and faithful Christian is one who lives the gospel in everyday life, not one who only reads about it or tries to manipulate God to fit his or her particular needs.

In the Western Model of Spirituality the idea was often communicated that God will always reward us in this life for our good deeds. This amazing piece of ignorance or misreading of the gospel justifies the belief of some Christians that as a reward for their faith in Jesus Christ, they will be well-to-do and never have to worry about anything, that all their undertakings will be blessed with worldly success, and that trials will never come their way. What book of Scripture supports such a belief? This popular notion affirms that if we initiate good works such as giving alms, God will reward us here and now as well as in heaven. We will own a nice house, enjoy great professional or business success, and work marvels in our ministry. The Scriptural Model offers no such promises. In fact, the Beatitudes, which express the ideal of happiness as Jesus presented it, teach that the happiest people are those who are persecuted for justice' sake. The reward of the hundredfold promised by Jesus to those who give up anything for his sake is not on the level of material success. The hero of the psalms is clearly the person who suffers affliction for the sake of God. The needy, the poor, the oppressed, the afflicted, are the constant concern of the psalmist and presented as the apple of God's eye. The psalms and writings of the prophets of Israel reveal the divine concern for the welfare, protection, and deliverance of those who suffer any affliction for God's sake.

The fourth disposition that the Scriptural Model of Spirituality presents is the need to cultivate the love of God here and now rather than to work for future reward or to pile up heavenly guarantees. The whole syndrome of reward and punishment is a disposition toward God that springs from an attitude that is normal for children but should develop into a more mature attitude in adults if their religious education is truly adequate. The best way to impart a truly religious education is to communicate to students a personal discipline of prayer and the practice of virtue that enables them to understand the contemplative dimension of the gospel, which is to be guided by the inspirations of the Holy Spirit both in prayer and action.

Instead of worrying about guarantees for the future life, we need to trust God and believe that if we do what we can to love and serve God and our neighbor in this life, God will take care of the future. Why desire a future that God does not want for us? We must seek God more and more in the present moment, which is in fact the only place where God can be found. Since God is eternal, God is not to be found in the future but in the present. A suitable discipline should concentrate on the work that we can do now to develop mature Christian attitudes, especially a relationship to the Ultimate Reality whom Jesus calls *Abba*, "Father." *Abba* is passionately concerned for every creature, especially human beings, who are called to manifest God's goodness more than any other aspect of creation.

God is part of the human adventure. Through the Incarnation, God manifests his identification with the human condition just as it is. Our attitude toward God has to be governed by that revelation and not by some philosophy or by some scientific discovery that might change in the next generation.

This generation has finally been delivered by the Second Vatican Council from the destructive teaching called Jansenism, a distortion of the gospel and one of the heresies that insinuated itself into seminaries and the mainstream of Catholic teaching. Jansenism taught that the body is totally corrupt and that the salvation brought by Jesus Christ was not universal. The symbol of the latter doctrine is the crucifix with the arms of Jesus lifted straight above his head, indicating that he was not embracing the whole world, but only a chosen few. This negative view of human nature as hopelessly corrupt led to the practice of extreme penances. The doctrine took hold in France and spread throughout Europe through the emigrés fleeing the French Revolution. It infiltrated Irish seminaries and eventually came to America through immigrant priests. This pervasively distrustful attitude toward human nature, together with a pathological fear of God, dominated most Catholic educational institutions prior to the Second Vatican Council, long after Jansenism was condemned by the ecclesiastical authorities.

The attitudes of the Western Model of the self-outside-of-God tended to produce caricatures of God. In childhood we may have picked up these wrong attitudes toward God from parents or teachers. Well-intentioned but ill-conceived religious instruction can make God seem like a tyrant demanding instant obedience to his will, however arbitrary. Through myths and fairy tales, children know what tyrants are. A child who sees God as a tyrant is not going to want to go anywhere near him unless forced to do so.

Another attitude that may be communicated to a child is that of God as an implacable judge whose gavel is ever poised to bring down the verdict of guilty. Here again God is presented with intense overtones of fear or even terror. A third attitude is that of a policeman always on our trail, always on the watch to catch us in the least fault. Whenever this child thinks of God, off goes the emotional judgment that says, "This God, whatever they say about him in church, is dangerous. He is a tyrant, a policeman always on my trail, and a judge, ever ready to condemn me to eternal hellfire."

These attitudes persist. Even theological training may not affect the emotions that have recorded the programming of early life and substantially condition one's capacity to hear the teaching of the gospel. This belief system is like carrying a ball and chain around our feet. God has to go to incredible lengths to dissipate these unhealthy ideas, all of which could have been avoided if children were encouraged to develop a relationship of trust toward God, which parents and teachers, by their goodness and care, should model and nourish. The vocation of parents is to manifest in daily life the kind of love that God has for their children. That is surely one of the principal graces of the sacrament of matrimony.

There *is* a genuine fear of God, but this is designed to alert people with dispositions that are cruel or malicious to the realization that there will be an accounting for violence, oppression, and every kind of premeditated malice. But once anyone has been converted to God and has begun the spiritual journey, fear is useless, while faith expanding into boundless confidence in God is life-giving. In actual fact, "Fear of God" is a technical term in the Old Testament meaning "the right relationship with God." It does not refer to the emotion of fear, which automatically gives rise to the bodily reactions of fight or flight. The emotion of fear tends of its nature to keep one as far away from God as possible. Trust grows through efforts to serve God out of love and to deepen the relationship. This cannot be accomplished if we are afraid of God.

The spiritual journey has great difficulty in getting off to a good start if we are carrying a load of unexamined and unquestioned negative attitudes toward God. Our basic attitudes toward God are frequently solicited by circumstances and temptations to regress to former levels of relating that were childish and unworthy of God. We easily make judgments about God that are actually projections of our childish levels of consciousness. We also project on God the models of authority that we saw around us. If we had a dominating and authoritarian father, then God is easily felt to be dominating and authoritarian. If these influences were horrendous, then it becomes more difficult later in life to relate to God as God. Recognizing childish attitudes toward God and laying them aside will enable us to re-evaluate our relationship with God and to consider the possibility of making friends.

Chapter 3

The Theological Basis of Centering Prayer

WHERE DOES CENTERING PRAYER COME FROM? Its source is the Trinity dwelling within us. It is rooted in God's life within us. I don't think that we reflect about this truth nearly enough. With baptism comes the entire uncreated presence of the most holy Trinity: Father, Son, and Holy Spirit. We participate as human beings in God's life just by being alive, but much more through grace. We participate in the movement between the Father giving himself totally to the Son, and the Son giving himself totally to the Father. They empty themselves into each other. The Spirit of Love reconstitutes them, so to speak, so that they can keep surrendering forever. This stream of divine love that is constantly renewed in the life of the Trinity is infused into us through grace. We know this by our desire for God. That desire, however it may be battered by the forces of daily life, manifests itself in the effort that we make to develop a life of prayer and a life of action that is penetrated by prayer.

The Trinitarian life is manifested in us primarily by our hunger for God. Centering Prayer comes out of the life of God moving within us. Hence it is Trinitarian in its source. Its focus is Christological. It establishes us in a deepening relationship with Christ. Begun in Lectio Divina (the prayerful reading of Scripture) and other devotions and especially in the sacraments, our relationship with Christ moves to new depths and to new levels of intimacy as we grow in the practice of Centering Prayer.

Finally, Centering Prayer is ecclesial in its effects; that

is, it bonds us with everyone else in the Mystical Body of Christ and indeed with the whole human family. There is really no such thing as private prayer. We cannot pray at this deep level without including everyone in the human family, especially those in great need. We also feel the need to express this sense of bonding and unity with others in some form of community.

Let us look at each one of these points in detail. Centering Prayer comes from an existential relationship with Christ as our way into the depths of the Trinitarian relationships. As we sit in Centering Prayer, we are connecting with the divine life within us. The sacred word is a gesture of consent to the divine presence and action within. It is as if our spiritual will turned on the switch, and the current (the divine life) that is present in our organism, so to speak, goes on and the divine energy flows. It is already there waiting to be activated. Then as we sit in the presence of the Trinity within us, our prayer unfolds in relationship with Christ.

We know that Lectio Divina and our other devotional practices prepare us to relate to Christ. We go through a certain evolutionary process of acquaintanceship, friendliness, and friendship. The last implies a commitment to the relationship. Everyone knows very well the experience where we relate to an acquaintance whom we cultivate and get to know and gradually reach a place of commitment to him or her. Commitment is what characterizes friendship. We can walk away from casual acquaintances, but we cannot walk away from friendship once it has been established without breaking somebody's heart, including our own. Friendship with Christ has reached commitment when we decide to establish a life of prayer and a program for daily life tailored to getting closer to Christ and deeper into the Trinitarian life of love.

This is an important point. As we sit in prayer, we are not just juxtaposed to Christ. The movement inward to the Divine Indwelling suggests that our relationship with

Christ is an interior one, especially through his Holy Spirit who dwells in us and pours the love of God into our hearts. We are really identifying with the Paschal mystery. Without going through a theological reflection each time, it becomes a kind of context for our prayer, so that when we sit down in our chair or on the floor, we are relating to the mystery of Christ's passion, death, and resurrection, not as something outside of us but as something inside of us. That is why we experience fairly soon an identification with Christ in his temptations in the desert. Later we experience our identification with Christ in the garden of Gethsemane, and finally our identification with Christ on the cross. In our Christian perspective, Jesus has taken upon himself all the consequences of our sins and sinfulness, in other words, the false self with the accumulation of wounds that we bring with us from early childhood and our childish ways of trying to survive.

As we sit, we may receive the consolation of the Spirit. But after several years of this prayer, we always find ourselves in the desert, because that is the way to divine union. There is no way of getting well from the wounds of our early childhood except through the cross. The cross that God asks us to accept is primarily our own pain that we bring with us from early childhood. Our own wounds, our own limitations, our own personality defects, all the damage that people have done to us from the beginning of life until now, and our personal experience of the pain of the human condition as we individually have experienced it—that is our true cross! That is what Christ asks us to accept and to allow him to share. Actually in his passion he has already experienced our pain and made it his own. In other words, we simply enter into something that has already happened, namely, our union with Christ and all that it implies, his taking into himself all of our pain, anxiety, fears, self-hatred, and discouragement.

It is all included implicitly in his cry on the cross, "My God, why have you abandoned me?" That is the big question. Here is God's son, the beloved to whom we are to listen — Christ who has based his whole mission and ministry on his relationship with the Father — and it has all disappeared. His disciples have fled. His message is torn to shreds. He stands condemned by the religious and Roman authorities. There is nothing left of his message, humanly speaking. Yet this is the moment of our redemption. Why? Because his cry on the cross is our cry of a desperate alienation from God, taken up into his, and transformed into resurrection. As we sit there and sweat it out and allow the pain to come up, we realize that it is Christ suffering in us and redeeming us.

Centering Prayer is focused on the heart of the Christian mystery, which is Christ's passion, death, and resurrection. Each time we consent to a new light on our weakness and powerlessness, we are in a deeper place with Christ. To have the lowest place is to be in the highest place in God's view. I cannot tell you why this is so. Perhaps it is just the way God is. Christ in his passion is the greatest teacher of who God is. Sheer humility. Total selflessness. Absolute service. Unconditional love. The essential meaning of the Incarnation is that this love is totally available. Centering Prayer is simply a humble method of trying to access that infinite goodness by letting go of ourselves. Consent to God's presence and action symbolized by the sacred word is nothing else than self-surrender and trust.

Notice how the theological virtues correspond to each one of the sacred contexts. We place our faith in the Divine Indwelling of the Trinity. We place our hope in Christ's passion, death, and resurrection and entrust our lives completely to him. By enduring the gradual awakening of self-knowledge, we express through patience our love of God in an eminent degree.

There is another aspect to the context in which we pray. As we sit at the foot of the cross, identifying with the man on the cross who endured all the consequences of our personal alienation from God, we are being healed of our emotional wounds and the wounds we may have inflicted on our conscience. Through moments of interior resurrection there may come a breakthrough into permanent resurrection as the false self finally falls away, giving us the habitual freedom of the children of God.

Bonding with others takes place as the love of the Spirit is poured forth in our hearts. We feel that we belong to our community, to the human family, to the cosmos. We feel at home in the universe. We feel that our prayer is not just a privatized journey but is having a significant effect in the world. We can pour into the world the love that the Spirit gives us in prayer. We can plead for the divine mercy for those parts of the world that are being torn to pieces by war and violence. We sympathize with God who is suffering wherever any suffering is going on. What is so terrible about war and violence is that God is being torn to pieces. God has so identified with our lives and with our deaths that Jesus could say, "What you do to the least of these little ones, you do to me." This violence has to be repaired. This is an imbalance that needs the kind of love that is born in interior silence as we let go of ourselves and allow God to be God in us.

The great privilege of contemplatives is that we are invited to share first in our own redemption by accepting our personal alienation from God and its consequences throughout our lives, and then to identify with the divine compassion in healing the world through the groanings of the Spirit within us. "The unspeakable groanings of the Spirit," as Paul calls them, are our desires to bring the peace and knowledge of God's love into the world. The love that is the source of those desires is in fact being projected into the world and is secretly healing its wounds. We will not know the results of our participation in Christ's redemptive work in this life. One thing is certain: by bonding with the crucified One we bond with everyone else, past, present, and to come.

In Centering Prayer, then, the humanity of Christ is not

ignored, as some critics claim, but affirmed in the most positive and profound manner. Centering Prayer presupposes a living faith that the sacred humanity of Jesus contains the fullness of the Godhead. Christ leads us to the Father, but to the Father as *he* knows him. In virtue of Christ's sacrificial death and resurrection, we participate by grace in Christ's divinity. We are invited to worship the Father in spirit and truth. This is to follow Christ into the bosom of the Father where, as the Eternal Son of God, he surrenders to the divine source from whom he eternally emerges — and returns — in the love of the Holy Spirit.

Chapter 4

The Christian Contemplative Tradition

O NE OF THE ENDURING LEGACIES of the Second Vatican Council was its call to return to the gospels and to biblical theology as the primary sources of Catholic spirituality. The Word of God in Scripture and incarnate in Jesus Christ is the source of Christian contemplation. The Incarnation of the Word is the insertion of God into the human family and the insertion of the human family into God in the person of Jesus Christ. The Father, the Son, and the Holy Spirit are together, in one nature, both the Ultimate Mystery and the Ultimate Reality. Their interior relationship of total giving and receiving is the divine life that Christ was sent to share with us.

The Fathers of the Church in their homilies frequently explained the Scriptures from a contemplative perspective, or, as it was called in those days, "in the spiritual sense." The spiritual sense was understood to contain much more than an allegorical interpretation of a particular text. It was rather an insight into the inherent nature of the divinely inspired texts that revealed levels of meaning that the Spirit, by strengthening one's faith through the gifts of wisdom and understanding, enabled the Christian gradually to perceive. The manifold gifts of the Spirit were believed to come into full exercise through the regular practice of prayer and the growth of faith into contemplation with its progressive stages of development.

For the first sixteen centuries of the Christian era, contemplation enjoyed a specific meaning. In recent centuries, the word has acquired other meanings and connotations.

To grasp the full import of this key word in Christian spirituality, it is necessary to know that it evolved out of two distinct sources, the Bible and Greek philosophy. To emphasize the experiential knowledge of God, the Greek Bible used the word *gnosis* to translate the Hebrew word *da'ath*, which implies a kind of knowledge involving the whole person, not just the intellect (e.g., Ps. 139:1–6).

St. Paul also used the word *gnosis* to refer to the knowledge of God proper to those who love God. He constantly prayed for this intimate knowledge for his disciples as if it were an indispensable element for the complete development of Christian life (see Eph. 3:14–21; Col. 1:9).

The Greek Fathers, especially Clement of Alexandria, Origen, and Gregory of Nyssa, borrowed from the Neoplatonists the term *theoria*. This originally meant the intellectual vision of truth that the Greek philosophers regarded as the supreme activity of the human person. While using this technical Greek term, the Fathers, steeped in their own spiritual roots, incorporated the meaning of the Hebrew word *da'ath*; that is, the experiential knowledge that comes through love. It was with this expanded understanding that *theoria* was later translated into the Latin word *contemplatio* and handed down to us by Christian tradition.

This tradition was summed up by St. Gregory the Great at the end of the sixth century. He described contemplation as "the knowledge of God that is impregnated with love." For Gregory, contemplation was both the fruit of reflecting on the word of God in Scripture and a precious gift of God. He called it "resting in God." In this "resting" the mind and heart are not so much seeking God as beginning to experience, "to taste," what they have been seeking. This state is not the suspension of all activity, but the reduction of many acts and reflections to a single act or thought to sustain one's consent to God's presence and action at the depths of one's being during the time of prayer.

The understanding of contemplation as the knowledge of God based on the intimate experience of God's presence remained throughout the Middle Ages. Ascetical disciplines (such as fasting, vigils, prolonged solitude, periods of silence, ascetical obedience, simplicity of lifestyle) and more spiritual disciplines (such as discursive meditation, affective prayer, veneration of icons, psalmody, chanting, the rosary) always included contemplation as part of their Christ-centered goal.

Lectio Divina is the most traditional way of cultivating contemplative prayer. A mainstay of Christian monastic practice from the earliest days, it consists in listening to the texts of the Bible as if one were in conversation with God and God were suggesting the topics for discussion. Those who follow the method of Lectio Divina are cultivating the capacity to listen to the word of God at ever deepening levels of attention. Spontaneous prayer is the normal response to their growing relationship with Christ, and the gift of contemplation is God's normal response to them.

The reflective part, the pondering on the words of the sacred text in Lectio Divina, is called *meditatio*, discursive meditation. The spontaneous movement of the will in response to these reflections is called *oratio*, affective prayer. As these reflections and particular acts of will simplify, one tends to resting in God or *contemplatio*, contemplation.

These three acts — discursive meditation, affective prayer, and contemplation — might all take place during the same period of prayer. They are interwoven. One may listen to the Lord as if sharing a privileged interview and respond with one's reflections, with acts of will, or with silence — with the rapt attention of contemplation. The practice of contemplative prayer is not an effort to make the mind a blank, but to move beyond discursive thinking and affective prayer to the level of communing with God, which is a more intimate kind of exchange.

In human relationships, as mutual love deepens, there comes a time when the two friends convey their sentiments without words. They can sit in silence sharing an experience or simply enjoying each other's presence without saying anything. Holding hands or a single word from time to time can maintain this deep communication.

This loving relationship points to the kind of interior silence that is being developed in contemplative prayer. The goal of contemplative prayer is not so much the emptiness of thoughts or conversation as the emptiness of self. In contemplative prayer we cease to multiply reflections and acts of the will. A different kind of knowledge rooted in love emerges in which the awareness of God's presence supplants the awareness of our own presence and the inveterate tendency to reflect on ourselves. The experience of God's presence frees us from making ourself or our relationship with God the center of the universe. The language of the mystics must not be taken literally when they speak of emptiness or the void. Jesus practiced emptiness in becoming a human being, emptying himself of his prerogatives and the natural consequences of his divine dignity. The void does not mean void in the sense of a vacuum, but void in the sense of attachment to our own activity. Our own reflections and acts of will are necessary preliminaries to getting acquainted with Christ, but have to be transcended if Christ is to share his most personal prayer to the Father, which is characterized by total self-surrender.*

Contemplative prayer, rightly understood, is the normal development of the grace of baptism and the regular practice of Lectio Divina. It is the opening of mind and heart — our whole being — to God beyond thoughts, words, and emotions. Moved by God's sustaining grace, we open our awareness to God, who we know by faith is within us, closer than breathing, closer than thinking, closer than choosing — closer than consciousness itself. Contemplative prayer is a process of interior transformation, a relationship initiated by God and leading, if we consent, to divine union.

Contemplation is distinguished by some authors into

Kenosis, or self-emptying as it is described in the powerful words of Philippians 2:5–10.

kataphatic and *apophatic,* sometimes also known as the *via positiva,* or "positive way," and the *via negativa,* or "negative way." This distinction, insofar as it suggests opposition between the two, is misleading. *Kataphatic contemplation* is rather a preparation for contemplation. It is the affective response to sacred symbols and a disciplined use of reason, imagination, memory, and emotion in order to assimilate the truths of faith and to develop a personal relationship with Christ. It includes such practices as visualization meditation and the veneration of icons.

Apophatic contemplation is a further stage in that relationship. It is resting in God beyond the exercise of particular acts, except to maintain a general loving attention to the divine presence. It can take different forms according to the different persons who receive this gift. It would be helpful to reserve the term "contemplation" to this type of prayer.

In this context, it is important to correct the serious misapprehension that apophatic contemplation consists in pondering the total unknowability of God. The "unknowability" of the apophatic path does not mean "pondering an unknowable God," but rather, *not pondering at all* — simply resting in God beyond our ordinary human faculties of thinking and feeling. Different faculties are involved, which *do* apprehend a God who is present, but on a more subtle level of awareness. Traditional Christian teaching has referred to these faculties as "the spiritual senses."

The "unknowing" of the rational intellect in apophatic contemplation is an important bridge in East/West dialogue because it allows us to form a common language of experience without which dialogue about the higher states of consciousness is virtually impossible. It is also a way home for many Christians who have gone to the East in search of spiritual wisdom and who, upon hearing that there is a Christian contemplative tradition that knows something about experiencing God at a deeper level than our thoughts and feelings, have been able to return to the religion of their youth.

Along these lines, we might take note briefly of another source of confusion and controversy for the contemplative tradition, which comes from St. Teresa of Avila's teaching that one should never omit the thought of the sacred humanity of Christ no matter what state of contemplative prayer one has received. Since the whole essence of contemplative prayer is to move beyond thought, her teaching seems to call into question the legitimacy of apophatic contemplation as an appropriate practice for Christianity, and that is how it has sometimes been interpreted: to put the brakes on the natural transition from discursive meditation to contemplative prayer.

The development of a personal love of Christ is certainly at the heart of the Christian spiritual journey, but can this love be expressed only through *thought?* Teresa, who herself knew the contemplative terrain deeply and ecstatically, may have been reacting to certain exaggerations in her time — a distorted personal mysticism that loses touch with Christ's vision of the Kingdom as grounded in compassion for the suffering and the poor. In any case, methods of prayer that are not inspired by the gospel should not be confused with the normal development of one's relationship with Christ and the more intimate dimension that contemplative prayer initiates: resting in the divine presence beyond thoughts and feelings.

Since "the love of God is poured into our hearts by the Holy Spirit," as St. Paul says, we, too, as contemplative prayer grows, participate more fully in this movement of grace. The divine presence becomes a fullness that no longer requires the stepping-stones of thoughts, feeling, and particular acts, at least not habitually. St. John of the Cross, a contemporary of St. Teresa and a fellow Doctor of the Church, in *The Living Flame of Love* (stanza 3, vv. 26 to 59), describes the great harm that spiritual directors can inflict if they dissuade those who are called by the Spirit to the state of waiting upon God with loving attentiveness from following this attraction. Once faith has revealed the mystery of Christ's humanity, one's attention during prayer is absorbed by the presence of the divine Person who dwells within it. One returns to daily life with this transformed consciousness, manifesting the fruits of the Spirit and the Beatitudes.

Contemplative prayer enjoys an ancient and venerable history within Christianity. This form of prayer was first practiced and taught by the Desert Fathers of Egypt, Palestine, and Syria, including Evagrius, John Cassian, and St. John Climacus, and has representatives in every age. In the patristic age: St. Augustine and St. Gregory the Great in the West, and Pseudo-Dionysius and the Hesychasts in the East. In the Middle Ages: St. Bernard of Clairvaux, William of St. Thierry, and Guido the Carthusian; the Rhineland mystics including St. Hildegarde, St. Mechtilde, Meister Eckhart, Ruysbroek, and Tauler; later the author of the *Imitation of Christ* and the English mystics of the fourteenth century such as the author of *The Cloud of Unknowing*, Walter Hilton, Richard Rolle, and Julian of Norwich. After the Reformation: the Carmelites, St. Teresa of Avila, St. John of the Cross, and St. Thérèse of Lisieux; among the French school of spiritual writers, St. Francis de Sales, St. Jane de Chantal, and Cardinal Berulle; among the Jesuits, Fathers De Caussade, Lallemont, and Surin; among the Benedictines, Dom Augustine Baker and Dom John Chapman; among modern Cistercians, Dom Vital Lehodey and Thomas Merton.

Over the centuries ways of cultivating contemplative prayer have been called by various names corresponding to the different forms they have taken. Thus we have Pure Prayer (Cassian), Prayer of Faith, Prayer of the Heart, Prayer of Simplicity, and Prayer of Simple Regard. In our time initiatives have been taken by religious orders, notably by the Jesuits and the Discalced Carmelites, to renew the contemplative orientation of their founders and to share their spirituality with lay persons. The Benedictine Dom John Main revived a method of cultivating contemplative prayer that he attributed to John Cassian. The method of Centering Prayer, based primarily on the fourteenth-century *Cloud of Unknowing* and the teaching of St. John of the Cross, is a further attempt to present the teaching of earlier times in an updated format and to put a certain order and regularity into it.

There are stages in the development of contemplation. St. Teresa describes them in *The Interior Castle*, beginning with the Fourth Mansion. St. John of the Cross also describes the development of contemplation and distinguishes two paths: the exuberant mysticism of St. Teresa and what he calls "the hidden ladder of faith." To him we owe a much clearer understanding of the important role of contemplative prayer in the development of faith, hope, and love. In his presentation of the spiritual journey, the faith that works through reasoning gradually grows in such a way that the usefulness of concepts and symbols disappears. Faith becomes purer and forms a stronger foundation for total trust in God and for the works of unconditional love.

All of this is more the work of the Spirit than that of the human person. In fact, growth in divine union carries with it the need to diminish our human activity and to learn to wait upon the Lord. It presupposes the gradual purification of the sense faculties in the night of sense and the spiritual faculties in the night of spirit. Thus, the essence of the contemplative path is not to be identified with psychological experiences of God, though these may occasionally occur. The essence of contemplation is the trusting and loving faith by which God both elevates the human person and purifies the conscious and unconscious obstacles in us that oppose the values of the gospel and the work of the Spirit. Contemplative prayer in the classic or strict sense of the term is "the narrow way that leads to life."

Chapter 5

The Process of Lectio Divina

L ECTIO DIVINA is the method of contemplative prayer that evolved in the monastic milieu. It is primarily a way of listening to the Scripture. The Christian community is essentially a scriptural environment. This is also what a parish is supposed to be. A monastery is a place where one is constantly immersed in a scriptural environment: the offices at different times of the day, solitude, places of silence, and a community of similarly minded people. In listening to the Scripture in the liturgy and reading it in private, there seems to be a dynamic inherent to the word of God that gradually moves one from one level of faith to the next.

The monks of the Middle Ages called these different levels the "four senses of Scripture." The senses of Scriptures are not four ways of discussing a particular text on a rational level. They are four levels of listening to the same passage. The teaching presupposes that Scripture contains a mysterious dynamic that moves one to ever deeper levels of understanding the word of God. These are the literal, the moral, the allegorical, and the unitive (sometimes known as the anagogical). Modern exegetes focus primarily on the literal sense of Scripture, seeking out the philological meaning of the words and the cultural background in order to understand how to interpret these words. This research is valuable for ferreting out more precisely what God was trying to say through the sacred writers. But that is not the purpose of Lectio Divina. Divine reading as the monks conceived it was not done for the sake of information but for insight. It was not to learn something but to encounter Christ. A friendship was developing.

Before printing was invented, there were only a few

manuscripts available. Monks would read one book of the Bible such as Isaiah or one of the gospels for a whole year. They were expected to learn the psalms by heart so that they could run blocks of Scripture through their memory all the time. When they gave time to Lectio, it was something special. They would start reading the Scripture and when something struck them, they would stop, reflect on the text, and then pray over it, asking God for the good things they read about. They would move from discursive meditation to affective prayer or aspirations of the will, then to repeating the same aspiration over and over again, and finally they would experience resting in God. This was the goal of the whole process. Some monks might spend most of the time with just a word or two, resting in the presence of God. The whole monastic environment, since it was so steeped in Scripture anyway, encouraged this movement toward contemplation. When you are constantly in contact with the word of God, you don't have to read extensively in order to be restimulated or to be restored to a state of recollection. The monks were more or less held in the presence of God by their environment and the structure of their lives.

Lectio Divina was not just a mental or purely spiritual activity. The monks of the Middle Ages used to whisper the words so that their bodies were engaged in the conversation. They would also read very slowly, the whole process of Lectio taking at times a couple of hours. In our day, we are almost completely desensitized to sacred reading because we are so used to newspapers, magazines, and speed reading. We tend to read the Scriptures as if they were just another book to be consumed. Lectio is just the opposite. It is the savoring of the text, a leisurely lingering in divine revelation.

What is so remarkable about the process of Lectio is that one can move from one level of relating to Jesus to the next in the same period of prayer, experiencing a variety of responses to the divine initiative. And gradually, as friendship with Jesus deepens, the "four senses of Scripture" begin to unfold as a dynamic within one's own life. The word of God is within us. It is an action, not just a statue inside us.

How does this dynamic work? The first, or literal, sense of Scripture is the historical message and example of Jesus. But when we engage the gospel through Lectio Divina, we begin to put what it says into practice. Augustine writes that we understand more by doing what it says than by how much of it we read. When we begin to put into practice and live by the Scripture, we have reached the moral sense. The message of Jesus is understood much more fully by putting it into practice than by reading and reflecting on the philological meaning of words, however valuable that study may be.

When the moral sense has been experienced for a while, a new realization begins to emerge. As we read the gospel and interiorize the events in which Jesus brings his disciples and friends to new levels of faith, we ourselves move beyond the moral sense into the allegorical sense of Scripture. It slowly dawns on us that the gospel is about *us*; that our own life is mirrored in its pages. The same sort of experience of God that we have encountered, now by grace, now in the mystery of the Spirit, was happening historically to those people who actually contacted Jesus and experienced his ministry. And this sense of mirroring applies not only to the New Testament, but to the Old as well.

When I came out of the novitiate in Valley Falls, Rhode Island, my confessor said, "You should read the whole of the Old Testament." I was more interested in reading St. John of the Cross at that time of my life, but being an obedient monk in those days, I said, "Sure," and I started with a heavy heart to read Genesis. That wasn't too bad. There are some wonderful stories in it. Then I picked up Exodus. I said, "Do I have to read this word for word?" I started reading it, and all of a sudden a mysterious light appeared, so to speak, on the other side of the page; the words started jumping out at me, and I got very excited. I said, "This book is talking about my life. Whoever wrote this book must have been my psychiatrist." Here I was reading about how the Israelites were murmuring against their leader, and this is what I was doing. They were going through the Red Sea and struggling with the slavery of sin, and that was the story of my own conversion. A few words would set off huge vistas of meaning and understanding; it became one of the most exciting books I ever read.

That is what the allegorical sense does to you. It enables you to identify your own personal spiritual journey with the events in the Old Testament that record salvation history: Noah, the passage through the Red Sea, crossing the Jordan — all those classical biblical events are made available in the sacraments and accessed through prayer. Salvation history is the same grace at work in us. It was present in the Old Testament, saving God's people in virtue of Christ's future coming. The fullness of grace was present in the gospel, and the fruits of that grace are treasured up in the sacraments of the Church. At the allegorical level, we are now listening to the voice of Christ speaking through the readings we hear in the liturgy, savor in Lectio Divina, and recognize in the events of our own lives. It is the same saving grace at work, just as available now as it was then, and more so. When you begin to experience this, you listen to the Scriptures in a very different way. They are not historical documents anymore, but stories about your own experience of the spiritual journey.

The fourth level of Scripture is the unitive (anagogical). That takes place when you are so immersed in the word of God that the word is coming out of you as a kind of continuing revelation. John Cassian wrote that one of the indications of the unitive understanding of Scripture is when you chant the psalms as if you were composing them. You have been assimilated to the word and vice versa.

One other aspect of the allegorical sense of Scripture should not be passed over. This is the unloading of the unconscious, or purification. Purification occurs when, because of the trust and honesty that develops toward God as a result of a lively identification with the texts of Scripture, we are able to confront the darker side of our personality. We begin to experience the biblical desert. The biblical desert is not a place, but a state in which we experience inwardly what the passage of the Israelites through the desert and other similar texts symbolize outwardly.

The allegorical level of Scripture involves the emptying of the junk in the unconscious — that is, the emotional damage that has been done to us from the moment we were conceived until now. Once we have cracked this shell of our ordinary psychological level of awareness with the help of contemplative prayer, we still have to work our way through or rather endure the spontaneous evacuation of all that emotional garbage. It has to be emptied out before the experience of divine union can be fully achieved and the true self can begin to motivate us rather than the false self, with its excessive demands and hidden agendas.

Notice the spiral movement of the four senses of Scripture. You are not just going around in circles. As you return to the same passage in Lectio Divina, it begins to take on new meaning. As you gradually interiorize the four senses of Scripture in your life, you come back to the same texts but at a higher (or deeper) level of understanding. This spiral motion is the way all aspects of the contemplative life develop. It is not a rocket that goes straight up. You keep coming back constantly to the same old routines, but they are not really the same because *you* change, even though nothing may change outwardly in your life. This is the invitation that Christ seems to be offering when he says, "He who has ears to hear, let him hear," implying that we could listen better if we could only listen deeper.

Remember the apostles on their way to Jerusalem when Jesus was trying to tell them about his passion and resurrection and they couldn't understand him at all? "Their minds were a perfect blank," Mark said. They didn't want to hear, and so they *couldn't*. One of the great obstacles to hearing the word of God is precisely our identification with the false self, with its habitual expectations, demands, or "shoulds" that just won't go away. Even when one commits oneself to God consciously, the healing of the unconscious does not really get underway until one accesses the allegorical level. Contemplative prayer hastens the process of evolution by enabling us to hear the word of God without wax in our ears — that is, to be empty of attachment to our own ideas, programs, and plans. How are we going to get to that point without some discipline? I don't think we can. Asceticism for its own sake, however, merely feeds the emotional programs and their pathology. A true asceticism must work on our unconscious motivation.

Contemplative prayer deepens the process of listening, and it does so by two experiences. One is the affirmation of our being at the deepest level, which comes through peace and spiritual consolation and enables us to entrust to God our whole story. Not that God doesn't know it already; he is just letting us in on the secret. Without trust in God, we cannot acknowledge the dark side of our personality, our mixed motivation, and our selfishness in its raw misery. Deep prayer increases our trust in God so that we can acknowledge anything and are not blown away by it. Without that trust, we maintain our defense mechanisms. We try to hide from the full light of that realization. Like Adam and Eve, we hide in the woods. On the other hand, as our dark side is confronted, it is removed. By our acknowledging it, God takes it away. The process of contemplative prayer is a way of releasing what is in the unconscious. The psyche has a need for evacuation the same as the body, and it does this as a result of the deep rest of contemplative prayer.

How does the dynamic of the word of God function? Take as an example the passage of the Israelites through the Red Sea. The literal meaning is the historical event in which the Egyptians allowed the Israelites to escape and then recanted. The Israelites crossed a swamp called the Red Sea.

The Egyptians in pursuit were all drowned when the waters swept over them. The Israelites escaped to sing a song of liberation on the other side. Then they spent forty years in the desert trying to reach the Promised Land.

The moral sense arises when we try to put behind us what Egypt represents, namely, the tyranny of sin. The allegorical sense emerges when we experience the desert inwardly — that is, purification, waiting for God, and the rebellions of human nature when it is confronted by the temptations of the desert. Finally, the unitive sense is the experience of actually reaching the Promised Land, the symbol of peace and divine union. The word "rest," or *quies* in Latin, has a classical meaning in Christian tradition. "Come to me all ye who labor and I will give you rest," is the famous invitation of Jesus. Mental and physical rest are great values. But a much deeper rest is found in freedom from the tyranny of sinful habits and compulsions. A still deeper rest is freedom from the roots of sin. Then one's emotions are no longer interested in those agendas of the false self but reverberate to the values of the gospel, finding joy in the practice of virtue and in freedom from the dark side of one's personality. Finally, the greatest rest of all is the rest of perfect love in which one can rest in the midst of the most intense activity since there is no draining of energy because of attachments or frustrations. With no emotional programs for happiness lurking in the unconscious to be frustrated, one can be motivated entirely by the will of God. The deepest rest comes from love.

Every time we move to a new level of faith, there is an initial experience of disintegration, distress, confusion, and darkness. If we are not forewarned about the spiritual journey, it feels like something has gone wrong — "Have I committed a secret sin?" This is the normal way that the present level of our understanding — our attitude toward ourselves, other people, and God — experiences that our life just does not work any more at that level. We are challenged or forced to move to a deeper level.

The transitional stage is always painful because we know only where we are now, and we are not always ready, especially in the beginning stages of that journey, to move into the unknown. What we know is better than what we don't know. We resist the moment of creative change.

What moves us from one level to another? That is the question. Is it something we do? According to the method of Lectio Divina, we just keep reading the Scriptures; that is all. We just keep listening, growing in trust, and growing in love as in any relationship. The Spirit who wrote the Scriptures is within us and enlightens us as to what the Scriptures are saying to us. The word is ultimately addressed to our inmost being. It starts with what is most outward and works toward what is most inward to awaken us to the abiding presence of God. When we are in the unitive understanding of Scripture, the outward word confirms what we already know and experience.

Within this dynamic of Lectio Divina we can sense the important role of contemplative prayer. In classic monastic practice, the spiraling movement of prayer within a single period of Lectio Divina — from discursive reflection on the word, to affective response, to resting in contemplation — seems to be the mysterious "drive shaft" in the larger movement through the four senses of Scripture, and particularly toward the allegorical and unitive levels where purification of the unconscious and the unitive state are experienced. In the normal development of Lectio, we move through the various stages of prayer without even thinking about them and without the self-conscious concern for our place in the spiritual journey, a preoccupation that tended to enter the tradition after the Reformation when the term "mental prayer" was invented. The term "mental prayer" does not appear in the literature prior to the sixteenth century.

In the way that history regularly deals with spiritual movements, people tended to get locked into categories. With the tendency to analyze that was so characteristic of the late Scholastic Middle Ages, the spontaneity of the spiritual journey got lost, and the final stage of Lectio, resting in God — the purpose of all the other stages — tended to be left out. One was expected to do spiritual reading and discursive mediation for x number of years; if one lived to be very old — or maybe on one's deathbed — one might hope for an experience of contemplation. But in actual fact one rarely or never expected it and hence did not take steps to prepare for it. As a consequence, it got to be more and more identified as a form of prayer that belonged exclusively in a cloister — and not even commonly there. The integral link between Lectio and contemplation was broken.

That link needs to be restored. The two practices grew up as one in Christian tradition and organically nourish each other. The experience of resting in God when Lectio moves to contemplation invites the emergence and healing of the unconscious. This in turn paves the way for us to listen and respond to the gospel at ever deeper levels of our being.

Chapter 6

Will and Intention
in Centering Prayer

S T. JOHN OF THE CROSS WROTE, "The Father spoke one word from all eternity and he spoke it in silence, and it is in silence that we hear it." This suggests that silence is God's first language and that all other languages are poor translations. The discipline of Centering Prayer and the other traditional practices are ways of refining our receptive apparatus so that we can perceive the word of God communicating itself with ever greater simplicity to our spirit and to our inmost being.

The practice of Centering Prayer, therefore, is not contemplation in the strict sense of the term but a preparation for it. In the broad sense of the term, it might be called the first step on the ladder of contemplative prayer. As a rule we do not know when our prayer becomes contemplation in the strict sense. We only know that we are moving in this direction through our practice, and that the Spirit is moving toward us (see Diagram 1). As our practice becomes more habitual, the action of the Spirit's gifts of wisdom and understanding become more powerful and gradually take over our prayer, enabling us to rest habitually in the presence of God. This experience is not necessarily felt during prayer, but is experienced in its effects in daily life. Waiting on God in the practice of Centering Prayer strengthens our capacity for interior silence and makes us sensitive to the delicate movements of the Spirit in daily life that lead to purification and holiness.

In this practice our activity has a part, but it is an extremely gentle one. Our contribution begins by being

Diagram 1

THE DYNAMICS OF CENTERING PRAYER

(How it gradually evolves toward contemplation under the inspiration of the Holy Spirit.)

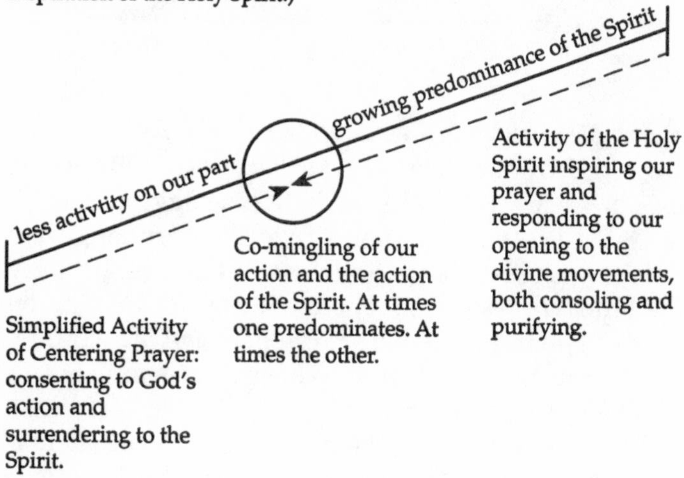

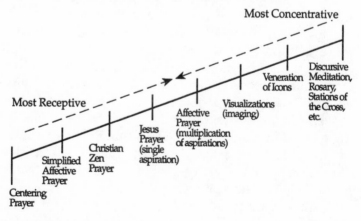

growing predominance of the Spirit

less activity on our part

Simplified Activity of Centering Prayer: consenting to God's action and surrendering to the Spirit.

Co-mingling of our action and the action of the Spirit. At times one predominates. At times the other.

Activity of the Holy Spirit inspiring our prayer and responding to our opening to the divine movements, both consoling and purifying.

Diagram 2

METHODS OF PRAYER THAT PREPARE FOR CONTEMPLATION

Most Concentrative

Most Receptive

Discursive Meditation, Rosary, Stations of the Cross, etc.

Veneration of Icons

Visualizations (imaging)

Affective Prayer (multiplication of aspirations)

Jesus Prayer (single aspiration)

Christian Zen Prayer

Simplified Affective Prayer

Centering Prayer

minimal and finishes by being almost imperceptible. The principal practice in Centering Prayer is to choose a word that represents our intention to consent to God's presence and action within us — it could be "God," "Abba," "Jesus," "peace," or some other word — and to return to that word whenever we feel our intention growing fuzzy.

Centering Prayer is probably the most receptive of the practices designed to facilitate the movement toward contemplation. What do I mean by "receptive"? In Diagram 2 our activity in Centering Prayer is represented at one end of a continuum in which various receptive and concentrative practices are shown on a scale. Centering Prayer is not a concentrative practice, nor an exercise of *attention*. It is an exercise of *intention*. It is our will, our faculty of choice, that we are cultivating. The will is also our faculty of spiritual love, which is primarily a choice. It may be accompanied by sentiments of love but does not require them. Divine love is not a feeling. It is a disposition or attitude of ongoing self-surrender and concern for others similar to the concern God has for us and every living thing.

Note that Centering Prayer is an acceptance not only of God's presence, but also of God's *action*. Our experience during a period of prayer (or even outside it) needs to be understood in the context of our relationship to the Spirit, which is primarily therapeutic. Why? Because we are sick! If we think we are well and experience this medicinal activity (the traditional term is "purgative"), it may cause us great surprise. Sometimes, instead of the blissful quiet we might expect from resting in God, we encounter turbulent movements from our unconscious, including strong emotions and even tears. Our growing trust allows us to see this as part of the process and to submit to it. Some medications can be painful, not because that is the desire of the doctor, but because our illness is such that it needs a serious remedy.

The will is developing the habit of surrender to God's increasing presence and action. Meanwhile, the Spirit's influence is also increasing in our prayer. We might imagine it as coming toward us as in Diagram 1. As our practice of Centering Prayer deepens, there is an interaction in which sometimes our own gentle activity predominates, and, at other times the Spirit takes over.

In this latter experience we may find what St. Teresa of Avila describes in *The Interior Castle* as the states of prayer, which she calls infused recollection, the prayer of quiet, union, and full union. They are levels of absorption of the faculties that are perceived by the one who receives them as the activity of the divine presence. In those situations we are more or less aware of God's action. The divine action can be just as present, however, at an even more intimate level, so intimate in fact that the various faculties cannot interpret or translate it into experience.

Just because one receives the spiritual consolation of the prayer of quiet or is completely absorbed in God in the prayer of union does not mean one is a saint. Since the Spirit's action is therapeutic, it may mean we are so sick that we need special attention! So we should not get puffed up by such things. On the other hand, we do not resist them either, because they may be just what is needed for our healing. In deep therapy, the first thing we have to do in order to be healed is to experience transference with the therapist. This is a mysterious emotional process in which we identify with the therapist and transfer to that person our relationship with authority figures from early life. Then the therapist can reflect back the acceptance we might not have felt as a child. This acceptance can heal the emotional privation of thinking of ourselves as unlovable. As fragile people, we need the experience of another person fully accepting us on the emotional level. Otherwise it is difficult to have a full self-identity or, as the psychologists call it, a strong ego, a valuable asset for the spiritual journey.

It is this self, even with much of the woundedness still remaining from early childhood, that we offer to God. Some people have been so deprived that they have an emotional conviction not only of being unlovable, but even of being a mistake. This is the source of the disease of self-hatred that is epidemic in our culture. This disease has to be healed in some degree for the spiritual journey to develop because the spiritual journey is the surrender of ourselves and of our self-identity. If we don't have a self or self-identity, we don't know what to give.

The affirmation of spiritual consolation and periods of peace and refreshment are a kind of transference with God. God then reflects back the acceptance and affirmation that our parents may have knowingly or unknowingly denied us in early childhood because of their own wounds from early life. If we can get over our self-hatred and the wounds of early childhood, we will make a tremendous contribution to the next generation. Unfortunately, parents do not usually discover their mistakes until the children are grown up. But please don't have guilt feelings on this point because the same melodrama has been going on since Adam and Eve. Such is the human condition. The right response is to accept our failures, work with them, and try to grow out of them. This down-to-earth process is an important aspect of the spiritual journey. Modern psychological discoveries can be helpful in our understanding of what the human condition really is from a diagnostic perspective. It is a pathology.

As the Spirit becomes predominant in our prayer, the use of the sacred word or sacred symbol during the time of Centering Prayer becomes less and less necessary or important. As long as we find that we are attracted to thoughts or feelings going by on the level of our memory or imagination, we freely make use of the sacred word not to push the thoughts away, but to reaffirm our original intention of consenting to God's presence. Some people who are visually oriented prefer to use a sacred symbol such as an image of oneself resting in the arms of God or of being under the loving gaze of God. Following the breath is another accepted practice, with particular appeal for those already introduced to breath practices in Eastern methods of meditation. But again, note that in Centering Prayer one does not pay attention *to* these symbols, but uses them only as the expression of our intention. As with the sacred word, they are used to focus *intention,* not as objects of attention and still less of *concentration.*

The sacred word or sacred symbol is something like the focusing apparatus on a video camera. If I were panning an audience, I would have to adjust the lens a bit for those up front, but those in the middle would then get fuzzy. To pan those in the middle I would have to adjust the lens again to get them in focus, and once again for those in the rear.

In the above analogy we are talking about physical clarity, but I am thinking in a different context here. The focusing process that the sacred word serves is not to bring a particular face, object, or symbol into focus in the imagination, but to focus our *intention* when it gets fuzzy. Intention is the most important factor in any contemplative prayer practice, but especially in Centering Prayer, in which our only activity consists in maintaining our intention to consent to God's presence and action during the time of prayer.

The intention becomes fuzzy when we are pulled back to our ordinary level of awareness by attraction or aversion to some thought, feeling, or impression. Usually this happens because that thought has stimulated one of the emotional programs for happiness in the unconscious. We all have them; they are a legacy of our childhood and infancy. Even after we have consciously rejected a childish attitude or behavior for the sake of the gospel, the influence of the emotional program may still be present in the unconscious — as for example, if one has a great emotional investment in the security symbols of a particular culture. The pain of our insecurity may have been so unbearable in early childhood that we repressed into the unconscious the very memory of the privation. But the unconscious remembers. The emotions are energy, and they don't go away if repressed. They are stored in the body. The body is the storehouse of emotional energy that is not adequately processed. As a result, one develops blockages to the healthy flow of energy in the body and nervous system. This reinforces the need for compensatory activity to hide the pain. Addictions are the ultimate way of distracting oneself from the emotional pain one is unwilling to face.

The spiritual journey from this aspect is a course in growing up and becoming liberated from childhood fixations at emotional levels that have become disruptive of our adult life and that interfere with our relationships. The journey is a form of divine psychotherapy in which God tries to heal us on every level, beginning normally with the body and the emotions.

For each level of emotional intensity there is a corresponding set of almost endless commentaries that are prerecorded in our memory bank. When a strong emotion is aroused, one is instantly besieged by a surge of commentaries, all of which take one farther and farther out of the peace, calm, and detachment that contemplation requires. That is why we need to have a focusing apparatus when our consent to God's presence and action begins to get fuzzy because of thoughts going by on the surface of our awareness that stimulate the programs in the unconscious. In Centering Prayer terminology, we liken these thoughts to boats passing by on the surface of a river (see Diagram 3).

It is not our attention that needs adjusting, because attention is secondary in Centering Prayer. We are not attending to a particular thought or object, or even to the sacred word as would be the case in a mantric kind of prayer. Our attention is a general and loving awareness of the presence of God. The actual work of Centering Prayer is consenting to God's presence and in doing so letting go of the present moment with its psychological content. If a thought or feeling stirs unconscious programs along with their commentaries, then before we "get on the boat," we

Diagram 3

THE RIVER

(As a metaphor of human consciousness)

Ordinary level of consciousness

The stream of consciousness resembles a river flowing toward the sea. The surface of the river stands for that level of consciousness that we use to attend to daily life. Sense perceptions, feelings, images, memories, reflections, and commentaries flow along the surface of our awareness like boats on a river. This is the ordinary level of **consciousness**.

The river itself stands for the **spiritual level of consciousness**. By practicing a discipline of prayer like Centering Prayer, the mind is less dominated by external events and our emotional reactions to them. Through the cultivation of our spiritual faculties of intuition and the will-to-God, we begin to experience the awakening of spiritual attentiveness.

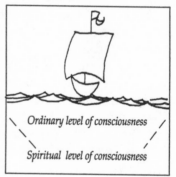

Ordinary level of consciousness

Spiritual level of consciousness

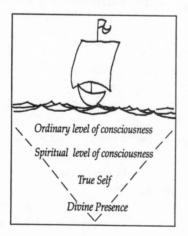

Ordinary level of consciousness

Spiritual level of consciousness

True Self

Divine Presence

The depth of the river stands for the **True Self** and the **Divine Presence**, the source from which our life emerges at every moment.

return to the sacred word. With time, patience, and many failures, we develop the habit of letting go of thoughts promptly — not by thinking about the fact that we are thinking, but simply by returning ever-so-gently to the sacred word. If you find yourself on a boat, just get off. There should be no self-recriminations, no sighs, no annoyance that you have had a thought. Any such reflection is another thought, another boat.

This prayer recommends itself as a prayer of great simplicity, a simplicity characteristic of childhood, which is to be present to the present moment and to forget what happened before. That is why the mood changes of children are so striking. They go from tears to laughter in an instant. Just the consent to return to the sacred word is all the activity that is required in Centering Prayer. Any analyzing, commentaries, guilt feelings, or recriminations are more distracting than the original thought. The original thought may simply have been a plan for the future or a memory. It is not nearly as effective in taking you out of interior silence as a feeling or an emotionally charged thought such as shame or guilt.

In this prayer we need to develop a certain joyful acceptance of our thoughts. We can't avoid them all. If we could, we would already be perfect in contemplation. I presume if that were the case, you would not now be reading this book. If you are like 99.9 percent of the human race, this is a process that is going to take some time and may not even be completed in this lifetime.

Contemplative prayer is a kind of purgatory. Purgatory in Catholic theology is a state in which we complete the journey to divine union in the next life if we have not quite finished it here. Every bit of progress means an enormous benefit for us and for everyone else in the human race. To be on this journey is really the greatest contribution one can make to the human family. This journey does not just involve what happens in prayer; rather, what happens in prayer enables us to live daily life as a continuation of the

---

GUIDELINES FOR CENTERING PRAYER

1. Choose a sacred word as the symbol of your intention to consent to God's presence and action within.

2. Sitting comfortably and with eyes closed, settle briefly and silently introduce the sacred word as the symbol of your consent to God's presence and action within.

3. When you become aware of thoughts, return ever-so-gently to the sacred word.

4. At the end of the prayer period, remain in silence with eyes closed for a couple of minutes.

---

purification process. The ups and downs of daily life, including its very everydayness, are the arena in which the Christian journey takes place. God is in solidarity with our lives and deaths, just as they are. Perfection does not consist in feeling perfect or being perfect, but in doing what we are supposed to do without noticing it: loving people without taking any credit. Just doing it.

To sum up, we use the sacred word only as a focusing apparatus to bring our intention into full clarity, whenever, because of the weakness of human nature and the fact that the emotional programs for happiness in the unconscious are still active, we need some means of returning to our original intention — that is, consent to God's presence and action within us. With regular practice, we develop a certain ease in promptly letting go. We then enter into the cloud of unknowing, which develops through repeated small acts of consent. This means that we have dismantled the emotional programs sufficiently that we are alert to when they intrude and can return to our original intention much more promptly and, indeed, without necessarily returning to the sacred word or sacred symbol.

The movement established by introducing the sacred word as the symbol of our intention to be open to God's presence and action brings us little by little to the spiritual level of our being, or, to use another analogy, to a general attentiveness to the river of consciousness itself rather than to what is passing along the surface of the river. The sacred word is simply the symbol of our intentionality. There is no special word, therefore, that is better than another, except that some words should be avoided because they spark an association of ideas and the tendency to think about other matters. In this prayer we are developing the capacity to wait upon God with loving attentiveness. The loving character is expressed by fidelity to the practice and patience while doing it.

Chapter 7

The Sacred Symbol as a Gesture of Consent

A S WE SAW IN THE LAST CHAPTER, our consciousness can be likened to a river, with our thoughts passing like boats along its surface. The surface of the river represents our ordinary psychological level of awareness. But a river also has its depths, and so does our awareness. Beneath the ordinary psychological level of awareness, there is the spiritual level of awareness where our intellect and will are functioning in their own proper way in a spiritual manner. Deeper still, or more "centered," is the Divine Indwelling where the divine energy is present as the source of our being and inspiration at every moment (see Diagram 4). Personal effort and grace meet at the most centered or inward part of our being, which the mystics call the "ground of being" or the "peak of the spirit."

Many methods of meditation make use of "sacred words," but these words are used in different ways, aimed at different levels of our awareness.

The sacred word is a gesture of the consent of our spiritual will to God's presence in our inmost being. The word appears in our imagination but exercises no direct, quieting function on the level of our ordinary stream of consciousness. Rather, it only expresses our intention, the choice of our will to open and surrender to God's presence. This is the difference between Centering Prayer and a practice that utilizes some form of *attention*, as in looking at a candle, repeating a mantra, or visualizing some image. That is why we do not have to repeat the sacred word continuously. We only use it to maintain our intention of faith and love

66

Diagram 4

LEVELS OF AWARENESS

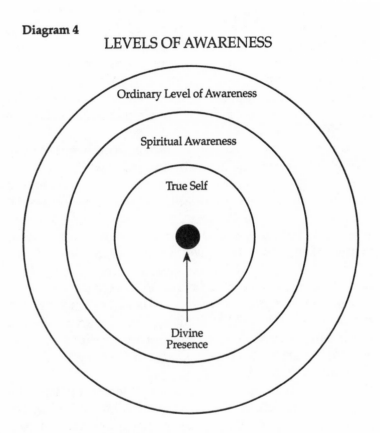

toward God. As long as thoughts go by like boats on the surface of the river without attracting our desire or causing an aversion, we do not need to return to the sacred word. In these instances, there is no interruption in the orientation of our *intention* toward God.

When we consent to the presence and action of God using the sacred word as a symbol of our intent, this movement of our will manifests itself very delicately in our imagination. The word does not have to be carefully articulated. It is neither reflected upon nor analyzed. It is simply a gesture or a symbol. Starting from one of the external senses (we can use a sacred gaze or breath as well), we move to the spiritual level and to the spiritual senses, which are analogous to the external senses. The sacred word comes from the heart and reverberates in the imagination only momentarily, whereas a mantra or a concentrative process is designed to slow down the flow of thoughts.

The primary function of the sacred word is not to push thoughts away or to thin them out. It is rather to express our intention to love God, to be in God's presence, and to submit to the Spirit's action during the time of prayer. It is only when one of the boats does not simply go by but attracts or repels us that we need to return to our sacred symbol. The reason is simple: when we are attracted to a particular thought, we have begun to lose the purity of our general loving intention to be in God's presence.

The sacred word, as we saw, is like a focusing apparatus on a camera, but the focus adjusts not an image but our intention. At the start of our prayer, we direct our general loving attention toward God, but there is no content. That is why it may be difficult for some to feel at ease with this practice at first. We let all particular thoughts go by without exception, no matter whether they are pleasant or painful or whether they bring spiritual consolation or a bombardment of thoughts and feelings. Occasionally, if we are bombarded by a particularly heavy siege from the unconscious, it may be difficult or impossible to return to the sacred word. Then we just sit with it, and the pain itself becomes our sacred symbol. Such surrender is still a deep consent to God's presence and action within. There will be more on this in Chapter 8.

All methods that lead to contemplation are more or less aimed at bypassing the thinking process. The reason is that our thinking process tends to reinforce our addictive process — our frenzy to "get something" from the outer world to fuel our compulsions or to mask our pain. If we can just rest on a regular basis for twenty to thirty minutes without thinking, we begin to see that we are not our thoughts. We *have* thoughts, but we are not our thoughts. Most people suffer because they think that they are their thoughts and if their thoughts are upsetting, distressing, or evil, they are stuck with them. If they just stopped thinking for a while every day as a discipline, they would begin to see that they do not have to be dominated by their thoughts.

Please remember that the term "thoughts" in our explanation of Centering Prayer includes not just concepts or images, but feelings, sense impressions from within and without, and even spiritual sensations. Every perception whatsoever goes under the umbrella of "thoughts."

The various methods that prepare for contemplation speak to the psyche in different ways. If we look at the whole spectrum of these varied forms of preparation, we can see that they range from receptive methods to concentrative methods. A concentrative method would be one in which we do much or all of the work — that is to say, when we constantly repeat a mantra, focus on our breathing, look at a candle or similar object, maintain a certain posture, or think about a Zen koan (an unresolvable conundrum). In a receptive method such as Centering Prayer, there is no attempt to focus attention. Our effort remains minimal.

Some methods are more concentrative; others are more receptive (see Diagram 2, page 56). In Zen there is a particular practice that is quite close to Centering Prayer in that one just sits in the prescribed posture, paying no attention to thoughts. Maintaining the posture, at least in the beginning, requires some effort. Centering Prayer, which does not even require posture beyond "relaxed but alert," is about as far in the receptive mode as one can go.

It is intentionality that distinguishes Centering Prayer from other forms of prayer. The difference between attention and intention is a difficult distinction for people who are not doing Centering Prayer. They see the external similarities between Centering Prayer and other forms of meditation and think they must be the same.

In Centering Prayer, we are not even attending to the thoughts going by. Indeed we are abstracting from the whole level of our ordinary psychological awareness in order to cultivate spiritual awareness.

We all begin life as a single cell. This is our personal big bang, so to speak. But there is enough energy in the single cell to sustain the whole rest of our lives. Let us call that our inmost center, or the divine ground of our being (see Diagram 4, page 67). From that center unfolds the true self and the right manifestation of that energy. We know that for reasons we call the human condition, we are not in contact with our true self. In response to the pain that may go back to infancy, birth, or even prior to birth as some recent therapeutic practice suggests, we develop very early in life what is called the false self, which represses the true self and hides its potential from us. This false self interacts with our environment under the influence of pain and self-protectiveness with the net result that we experience ourselves most of the time dominated by external events and our emotional reactions to them. The false self is functioning when we are dominated by external events instead of acting with freedom.

Our ordinary psychological awareness is somewhat like being at a movie that is extremely engrossing. Being dominated by events and our emotional reactions to them is like being at a movie that is so good that we identify totally with the plot or with one or another of the characters and forget that we are in the theater. Similarly, we are most of the time out of touch with the spiritual level of our being and allow events to dominate us rather than choosing what to do with them. As we work on this process through Centering Prayer and recognize the dynamics of the unconscious, our spiritual faculties and true self are being liberated. That experience relativizes our emotional investment in symbols of happiness demanded by the false self.

The reason is we are beginning to experience inner peace, which is the happiness we *really* seek. In the practice of Centering Prayer, we encounter the same emotional reactions we had before, only now we *notice* them instead of blindly reacting to them. It is essential that we learn to recognize the tendencies of our false self if we want to be happy, because only in recognizing them can we change them. We do not have to analyze them; we just have to notice them and let them go.

As interior freedom develops, we become like people at a lousy movie who know that they can get up and leave anytime. We also know that we are free to stay. This is the difference between a spiritual practice that is working and one that has not yet begun. In a process that has not begun, we continue to allow ourselves to be dominated by other people, circumstances, and the inner dynamics that were set in place in early childhood and over which we did not have control. As we begin to practice, we know that we have to own these dynamics in order to move beyond them, become our true selves, and manifest all the creative possibilities that God has given us. As this realization grows in us, we begin to act from our center. The chief effect of Centering Prayer is to live from our center. This of course does not mean that we do not interact with the world. On the contrary, we interact better than before because we are not defending ourselves from people or circumstances, but living reality as it unfolds. Centering Prayer, then, is not just a method of prayer but initiates a process that involves the response of our whole being to the gospel and its values.

Chapter 8

The Psychology of Centering Prayer

F OR CENTURIES THE GREAT MODEL of spiritual growth in the Christian tradition has been the friendship of Christ. Friendship is a marvelous paradigm because it suggests confidence, love, and self-disclosure, all of which increase as friendliness develops into friendship and ever deepening levels of commitment. The paradigm of friendship, however, does not necessarily include the aspect of emotional illness that is so characteristic of the human condition. The friendship of Christ, of course, does include the reality of human weakness and need. One characteristic of love is that it reduces our defenses. When our defenses go down, the dark side of our personality emerges. One important aspect of a true friendship is the willingness to help each other process that material.

Here is another model that might be appropriate for our time, at least for the Western world, which has been so influenced by contemporary psychology. I call this paradigm for spiritual growth the "Divine Therapy." Therapy suggests a climate of friendship and the trust that a topnotch therapist is able to inspire, while at the same time emphasizing that we come to therapy with a variety of serious emotional or mental problems.

The human race, as a whole, is a sick species. According to the Roman Catholic tradition, only the Blessed Virgin Mary came into existence and remained emotionally undamaged. Most people are not aware of their illness or how very sick they are. They do not have an adequate diagnosis of the human condition in general or their own illness in particular. Hence they do not reach out for the kind of assistance that they need in order to recover.

One of the great strengths of the Twelve Step Program of Alcoholics Anonymous is that it emphasizes how serious one's illness actually is. Participants in AA know that their lives are unmanageable and will never become manageable unless they work the twelve steps. In actual fact, most humans suffer from the serious illness that Ann Wilson Schaef calls "the Addictive Process" — indeed, as high as 98 percent of the population in the Western world, according to some recent statistics. Personally, I have never met anyone from the other 2 percent! The addictive process as a psychological term parallels what theology in the Christian tradition calls the "consequences of original sin," only in much greater detail. The addictive process manifests itself according to circumstances and personality in one or another of the many addictions that can now be treated by various Twelve Step programs. The advantage of being an addict is that you know that you will never get well without help. Unfortunately, the average practicing Christian, because of a certain modicum of respectability, does not seem to know this. It is not until the addiction gradually gets so bad and all semblance of functionality breaks down that one finally recognizes it. The practical question for all of us is "How addicted *are* we?"

The consequences of original sin according to traditional theology are three: illusion, concupiscence, and weakness of will. Illusion means that although we are irresistibly programmed for boundless happiness in a way that is inherent to human nature, we do not know where true happiness is to be found. Concupiscence means that we seek happiness in the wrong places or too much happiness in the right places. And finally, if we ever reach the point of finding out where true happiness is to be found, our will is too weak to pursue it.

What is different about this teaching from the proclamation of the first step of the Twelve Step Program of AA that "my life is unmanageable"? If one accepts the traditional doctrine of the consequences of original sin, the freedom to manage one's life is severely limited. It is on the basis of complete helplessness apart from the grace of God that the whole idea of redemption rests.

Once we reach the bottom line of the diagnosis, "my life is unmanageable," we do not have to wait until things fall completely apart to recognize the seriousness of our illness. We can start at once by taking preventive therapy designed to heal the roots of developing addictive processes before they become full blown. The gospel addresses the human condition just as it is. "Repent" — that fundamental call in the gospel to begin the healing process — means "change the direction in which you are looking for happiness." The various orientations for happiness that we brought with us from early childhood are not working. They are slowly killing us. If we respond to the invitation to repent addressed to us so lovingly by the divine physician, we can begin at once to take advantage of the Divine Therapy.

Therapy, as we saw, implies both the relationship of friendship and the relationship of healing. Reading the gospel from the perspective of contemporary psychotherapy provides us with a detailed diagnosis of the disease. Contemplative prayer and action — life under the direct influence of the Seven Gifts of the Spirit (counsel, prudence, fortitude, reverence, wisdom, understanding, knowledge) — is the gospel program for human health, wholeness, and transformation.

Many of Jesus' parables and recorded sayings are basically directed at our unconscious emotional programs for happiness, which tear us apart by ever increasing demands that cannot possibly be fulfilled. A person dominated by an emotional investment in the instinctual needs for control, esteem, or security will absorb into these magnetic energy centers every new experience and interpret it from their perspective. If it satisfies, there is temporary delight; if it frustrates, lingering distress.

How did we get hooked into these programs in the first place? This question is still under investigation in our time. The world religions have projected various creation theories to account for the human condition universally experienced as seriously flawed. Now psychology and science are making their contributions. Developmental psychologists such as Piaget, and more recently John Bradshaw, have attributed the cause to failures of parental nurturance and emotional wounding experienced in early childhood. In his book *The Ego and the Dynamic Ground* (SUNY Press, 1988) transpersonal psychologist Michael Washburn hypothesizes a repression of the sense of oneness with the source of our being — what he calls the "dynamic ground" — as the first step in the process of developing a separate self-identity — a repression that starts us off on a desperate search for happiness that cannot possibly succeed. Whatever the cause, the source of true happiness is missing from our growing-up experience. The awareness of the divine presence is true security, true affirmation, and true independence, but that reassuring presence and pervading sense of bliss is missing from everyone's developing consciousness.

Without the reassuring experience of God the world is perceived to be potentially hostile. Since the need for happiness is so fundamental and so strong, we invest at a very early age in various substitutes. Our programs for happiness seek in vain to compensate for the absence of the sense of God's presence as the developmental process proceeds. The net result of our efforts to repress emotional pain or to compensate for it is the formation of the false self. The gospel invites us to recognize that the false self is a disease that can be healed and to accept Christ as the divine physician or, in the context of this paradigm, the Divine Therapist. The healing process is primarily the work of contemplative prayer, which, along with the homework of daily life, constitutes the Divine Therapy.

Let's look at what I am calling the Divine Therapy to

see if it truly responds to the illness of the human condition and its diagnosis both theological and psychological. Let's envision a period of Centering Prayer as a take-off point and enlarge it to include several years of regular practice. Centering Prayer as it becomes habitual is dominated more and more by the contemplative gifts of the Holy Spirit: knowledge, understanding, and wisdom. When we sit down in prayer, our psychological experience is something like that depicted in Diagram 5 (remember that we are telescoping the cumulative effect of several years of practice into a single prayer period.) When we introduce the sacred word, we institute a circular motion with four major moments. The first moment is when we introduce the sacred word (or the sacred gaze or breath) as the symbol of our consent to God's presence and action within us and gently establish an attitude of waiting upon the Lord with loving attentiveness. At first there may be an experience of endless thoughts filling our awareness. When we have been practicing for several years, this normally passes fairly quickly into a deep sense of quiet, refreshment, or rest. This is the second moment in the circular movement of Centering Prayer. "Rest" is the term for a wide variety of psychological impressions such as peace, interior silence, contentment, a sense of coming home, of well-being, and most of all, of God's presence.

Suppose this rest is so deep that at some point during prayer there are few or no thoughts passing by. Or one has a strong sense of the presence of God. The experience of deep rest, cumulative now since we are talking about a year or two of practice, automatically causes the body to rest, and indeed to rest in a greater degree than in sleep.

The feeling of deep rest, especially when it involves a deep sense of the divine presence, leads to a kind of psychological transference with God. That is to say, God becomes the therapist in the psychoanalytic sense in which we look to a therapist for the trust and love that we did not feel we received as a child from an important other,

Diagram 5

THE FOUR "MOMENTS" OF CENTERING PRAYER

(Representing the psychological dynamics of several years of practice, but which can also be experienced in a single prayer period.)

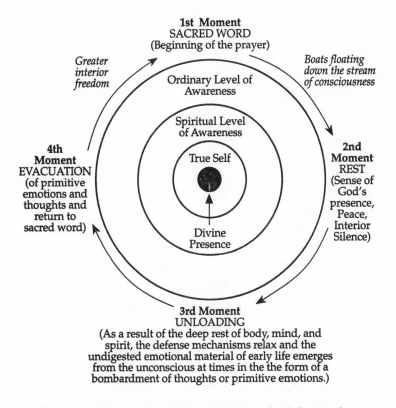

1st Moment
SACRED WORD
(Beginning of the prayer)

Greater interior freedom

Boats floating down the stream of consciousness

Ordinary Level of Awareness

Spiritual Level of Awareness

True Self

4th Moment
EVACUATION
(of primitive emotions and thoughts and return to sacred word)

2nd Moment
REST
(Sense of God's presence, Peace, Interior Silence)

Divine Presence

3rd Moment
UNLOADING
(As a result of the deep rest of body, mind, and spirit, the defense mechanisms relax and the undigested emotional material of early life emerges from the unconscious at times in the the form of a bombardment of thoughts or primitive emotions.)

Note: each cycle of the Four Moments begins at a level closer to the center (Divine Presence) because obstacles in the form of repressed emotional junk have been evacuated in the process. Thus the purification of the unconscious continues till divine union is discovered.

such as a parent. The pain of rejection, which the emotions have stored in the unconscious and which is reactivated by every new rejection in life, is projected onto the therapist, who reflects back the acceptance that we did not adequately experience in childhood. This heals the emotional wounds in a way that no amount of theological reflection can do. The emotions do not obey reason. They need reassurance in the area and in the measure in which they felt deprived. Almost everyone has a residue of emotional pain for the affection and security that as infants we needed and felt deprived of.

Deep rest is not only the result of freedom from attachments or aversions to thoughts, but also the feeling of being accepted and loved by the divine Mystery that we sense within us and that Christian doctrine calls the Divine Indwelling. In other words, our awareness of the divine presence begins to reawaken.

Rest grows deeper as our trust in God deepens, and the emotional doubts about our self-worth, impressed upon us in early childhood by various rejections or excessive competition with other siblings, begin to relax. Because the rest is so profound, the body rests as never before. The body is the storehouse of the emotional pain of early life as well as the consequences of trying to deal with that pain through coping mechanisms such as repression and compensatory activity. As a result, the hardpan of defense mechanisms around the emotional weeds of a lifetime begins to soften, the body's extraordinary capacity for health revives, and the psyche begins to release its waste materials. Our awareness during prayer becomes a channel of evacuation similar to the evacuation channels of the physical body. The psyche then starts to disgorge the undigested emotional material of a lifetime in what might be called an attack of "psychic nausea." Early emotional traumas were never fully digested, integrated, or evacuated because as infants and children we could not articulate our pain. We could not speak yet, or if we could, we did not have the language or the courage needed to express what we felt. Unarticulated emotional experiences that are traumatizing may be pushed into the unconscious where their energy remains. Emotions are energy. They can only be dissipated by acknowledging or articulating them.

I call this third moment in the circular movement of Centering Prayer "the unloading of the unconscious." "Unloading" refers to the experience of psychic nausea that occurs in the form of a bombardment of thoughts and feelings that surge into our awareness without any relationship to the immediate past. That lack of connection with the source of painful thoughts or feelings is what identifies them as coming from our unconscious. Evacuation of this primitive material is the fourth moment of the circle. Having carried this emotional pain for twenty or thirty years (or longer), the evacuation process may be extremely painful, but if it is prepared for by the discipline of a practice like Centering Prayer on a daily basis, then the trust in the Divine Therapist is there to enable us to handle it. We just have to put up with the turbulence; when it is possible to return to the sacred word, we return to it and start the circular process once again.

This unloading process may take place for some people rather soon after starting Centering Prayer, but usually not in a dramatic way. The Spirit seems to start from the outside and work inward. But if there is an outside stimulus, the process may be more immediate and intense. Tragedy, accident, or psychotherapy may have loosened up this material so that some of it may be close to the surface of our awareness. In this case, a single period of Centering Prayer might provide enough rest for this material to break through our defenses and to come to full awareness. Jesus makes a strong point in the gospel that the Kingdom of God is active precisely in circumstances that from our point of view are unacceptable. Just as Jesus befriended the outcasts of society, so he befriends us in these moments of psychological unloading and tries to reassure us that what has come to consciousness is for our healing and that seeing it is not going to kill us. Therapists, I presume, try to make their clients well, and sometimes this involves bringing up a painful issue. Every now and then the therapist gets tired of waiting for us and says, "Let's take up your distressing relationship with so and so." And we respond, "Let's wait until next week." Similarly, when the Divine Therapist suggests, "Let's take a look at that disturbing feeling and where it comes from," we get spooked and think there must be a better way of getting to heaven. We bury our noses in some devotional book or practice, in work, entertainment, or some other preoccupying activity in order to avoid facing the real issues. But if we persist in the practice of Centering Prayer, the real issues will reassert themselves, and eventually our growing trust in God enables us to endure the healing process. (Much the same dynamic occurs when two people truly love each other.)

Where are we after having made the full circle? We are never where we started because now we have unloaded that which was stuck somewhere in the body. We might conceive of God as our deepest center and our true self as a circle around it (see Diagram 4 on page 67). Our normal consciousness, as we saw, directs our attention to the circumference of our awareness where it is dominated by events and our reactions to them. Like someone at the movies, we get so absorbed in the story that we identify with the characters and may even forget that we are in the theater. Our normal psychological state is being dominated by life's events and our reactions to them. We do not realize that external events and other people influence our worldview and predispose our choices.

Centering Prayer practice is the reverse. It is like going to a bad movie where, because we do not identify with the actors, we know we are in the theater and can get up and leave any time. But if we are attached to preconceived ideas and prepackaged values, it does not occur to us to get up and leave. We have not yet awakened to the fact that at the level of our spiritual self we are only witnessing what is going on in our lives and are not captive to the plot.

Thus, to return to Diagram 5 (page 77), whenever a certain amount of emotional pain is evacuated, interior space opens up within us. We are closer to the spiritual level of our being, closer to our true self, and closer to the Source of our being, which lies in our inmost center but is buried under the emotional debris of a lifetime. We are closer to God because through the process of unloading we have evacuated some of the material that was hiding the divine presence. Thus, when in prayer we start the circular motion again, we are closer to our center. As a consequence, there is deeper rest. This inevitably causes more unloading of emotional junk — up it comes in the form of primitive emotions or emotionally charged thoughts that bear no relation to the recent past. When the storm subsides, we return to the sacred word. We are closer to our center as we start the process again. This circular movement of rest, unloading in the form of emotionally charged thoughts and primitive emotions, and returning to the sacred word is constantly bringing us closer to our center. So the circular motion in fact turns out to be a dynamic process resembling a spiral staircase.

The unloading process can manifest itself first in physical symptoms like a little pain somewhere in the body, a twitch, or an itch. An emotional knot that is close to the surface of the body may be unwinding. By temporarily directing one's attention to that place, the discomfort usually dissipates rather rapidly.

When a certain number of superficial knots have been evacuated through the deep rest of prayer, the Spirit goes to work on more interior stuff. We may then experience a flow of tears. Most people have repressed a lot of grief in their lives for cultural or personal reasons. Now the body feels for the first time the freedom to do what was previously denied it. Similarly, in the beginning of practicing Centering Prayer, if we are exhausted, the body calls for sleep. This is not the purpose of prayer, but the body, if it is allowed to do what it has been forbidden to do, feels much better. When we are sufficiently rested, we will not fall asleep so often — unless, of course, we continue making the same exhausting mistakes in our emotional lives.

As the emotions normalize, grief seems to be one of the first to be released, and that can bring a flood of tears. For cultural reasons men are a little slower than women at getting to this point. Tears are something that the early Desert Fathers prayed for because they had the insight to realize, without knowing the psychology of it, that tears open the heart, soften harsh feelings, and wash away bitterness. They are a precious gift. What is surprising for people, if they are not aware of this process, is that the tears do not come from any recent grief they can identify. To complete my discussion of Diagram 5, if we keep up our practice — and I emphasize *doing* it, not feeling it — the rest does the rest! We keep returning, resting, evacuating more junk, enjoying more interior freedom. If we live long enough, we will come to the Center.

What happens when we hit the Center? Since there is no more junk left to hide the divine presence, I presume we are in divine union. Faith believes that God is waiting for us. Such is the meaning of the Divine Indwelling. If we just keep up our practice, the divine presence cannot remain hidden forever.

To understand this process in its vertical dimension, I like to use the analogy of a middle Eastern tell, that archaeologist's delight (see Diagram 6). It seems that in ancient times when a city-state would overcome an adversary, the military would burn it down and build their own town on top of the old one. As a result, we find one civilization built on another in the same place. Tells were ignored for centuries because people thought they were just hills. Now they are considered archaeological treasures.

The first job for the archaeologists is to clean off the top of the tell and get rid of the weeds and rocks and un-

Diagram 6

THE ANALOGY OF THE TELL AND
THE ARCHEOLOGICAL DIG

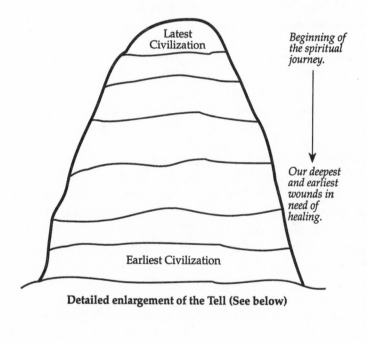

Latest
Civilization

*Beginning of
the spiritual
journey.*

*Our deepest
and earliest
wounds in
need of
healing.*

Earliest Civilization

Detailed enlargement of the Tell (See below)

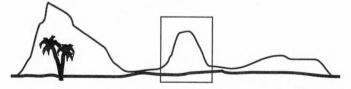

The Tell rising up from the plain.

earth the last civilization that thrived there. They throw out the ashes and debris and send the mosaics and pottery to the British Museum. Then they take time off, enjoy the reward of their discoveries, gather together some graduate students from some big university, raise money from some humanitarian foundation, and come back and dig up the next city-state. The process takes many years. Level by level, the archaeologists work down, culture by culture, all the way down to the stone age. As a result of this research we have a much more comprehensive view of the literal meaning of the texts of Scripture. Archaeologists have discovered sacred writings as well as business transactions, enabling scholars to reconstruct many aspects of those early civilizations.

I suggest that the Holy Spirit, as the divine archaeologist, works in a somewhat similar mode. She picks us up where we are now, whatever our chronological age. The first thing is to heal the most destructive aspects of our present relationships and addictive behaviors. As a result, we enjoy a certain freedom in practicing virtue and doing good to others. A personal relationship with Christ forms. We may experience enthusiasm for Scripture. Our devotional life, the sacraments, the liturgy, spiritual reading, ministry, all begin to flourish. This period is often called "the springtime of the spiritual journey." I suppose born-again Christians have a similar experience. The mistake would be to think that the journey is over. It has not even begun. This is just the first stage. But this stage is so delightful that people are reluctant to let go of it.

At some point, the Spirit may decide that the springtime has lasted long enough. In monastic life, we call it "the fervor of novices." The Spirit decides to dig down to the next level. Actually, the Spirit intends to investigate our whole life history, layer by layer, throwing out the junk and preserving the values that were appropriate to each stage of our human development. Without following an exact chronology, the Spirit seems to work back through the successive stages of our lives: old age (if we have arrived there), mid-life crisis, early adult life, late adolescence, early adolescence, puberty, late childhood, early childhood, infancy, birth, and even prebirth. The sequence corresponds in general to the *emotional* chronology of our psyche, in which the deepest and earliest wounds tend to be the most tightly repressed. Eventually the Spirit begins to dig into the bedrock of our earliest emotional life, where the feelings of rejection, insecurity, lack of affection, or actual physical trauma were first experienced. The most primitive emotions arise to consciousness because raw anger, fear, and grief were our only possible responses at that time. Hence, as we progress toward the center where God actually is waiting for us, we are naturally going to feel that we are getting worse. This warns us that the spiritual journey is not a success story or a career move. It is rather a series of humiliations of the false self. It is experienced as diminutions of the false self with the value system and worldview that we built up so painstakingly as defenses to cope with the emotional pain of early life.

This is a dynamic experience and cannot be captured exactly in these static diagrams, but there is one other diagram that might be helpful (see Diagram 7). The spiral staircase is a combination of the horizontal and vertical diagrams. The top of the staircase corresponds to our first conversion, the time when we first commit ourselves to a life of prayer. At that time we usually have to deal with some particular set of temptations, failures, addictions, or compulsions. The springtime of the spiritual journey lays that unmanageable situation to rest temporarily because of the new values that explode in a burst of spiritual enthusiasm. Flowers may cover a dung heap because of seeds that were dropped there. Our experience then will be of flowers rather than of what lies beneath. The movement from springtime into the real work of the spiritual journey takes place not on our initiative, because we probably would stay in our first fervor forever if we could. The Spirit as our lov-

Diagram 7

THE SPIRAL STAIRCASE

(Combining the horizontal and vertical diagrams in their dynamic unity.)

Transforming Union
Purity of love.

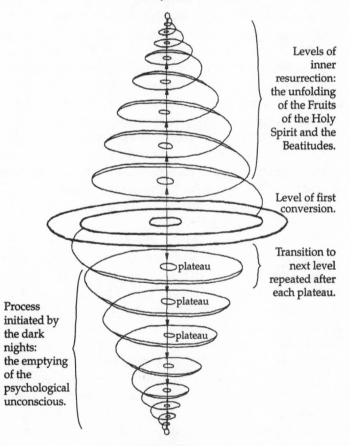

Levels of
inner
resurrection:
the unfolding
of the Fruits
of the Holy
Spirit and the
Beatitudes.

Level of first
conversion.

Transition to
next level
repeated after
each plateau.

plateau

plateau

plateau

Process
initiated by
the dark
nights:
the emptying
of the
psychological
unconscious.

Purity of heart
Transforming Union.

ing therapist invites us to look at the next level of our life and to see if that, too, can be rescued from its limitations.

At this point, the initial graces that were given to our rational faculties and emotions are withdrawn — a classic experience in the spiritual journey known as "the dark night of sense." Our enthusiasm for various devotional practices and activities disappears because God no longer gives the grace that works through the levels of reason and emotion. God, too, seems to withdraw, to our great distress or consternation. Instead of being present during our time of prayer, God seems not to show up anymore; it feels as if God could not care less. This is especially painful if the former relationship was very satisfying, exciting, or consoling. The thought rises, "God has abandoned me!" When the dryness is extreme, Lectio Divina is like reading the telephone book and spiritual exercises are just a bore. We are irritable and discouraged because the light of our life has gone out. It took so many years to find God and now God has gone away. There is a constant temptation to think we have done something wrong, but we can't figure out what it was. Our tendency is to project onto God the way we would feel in a similar deteriorating relationship with another human being, namely, hopeless. This judgment is most unfair to God. At this point a lot of people throw in the towel and decide, "The spiritual journey is not for me."

As the transition to the next layer takes place, there may be a discouraging sense that all is ending, and in a sense, it *is* the end of our world. But our world is not *the* world; it is just one of them. God cannot possibly go away. It is true, our relationship with God, if we deliberately walk away, can be injured for a while, but God does not really leave us. If God did, we would just disappear or turn into a grease spot, since God is the very life of our being.

Creation is ongoing. What God has done in this situation is simply to "go downstairs" to a more intimate place on the spiral staircase, where he is waiting for us to join him at a new level of maturity and trust. If we are very quiet in the night of sense, St. John of the Cross writes, we may notice a delicate sense of peace and may even begin to enjoy the more substantial food of pure faith. As we let go of the level on which we formerly found satisfaction, we move to a deeper level of faith, which is far more reliable and much more strengthening for the journey.

The Fathers of the Church allegorized this basic experience as the journey from Egypt to the Promised Land. The biblical desert is the symbol of the purification of the various stages of our personal life history. Purification is never the rejection of anything, but the sifting of the wheat from the chaff. It is a kind of judgment in which the Spirit sifts what was good from what was harmful at each stage of our development and gathers the wheat into barns while the limitations that were built into each stage of our early development are left behind. Thus the awe and wonder of the infant is recaptured; only the ignorance and tantrums of the child are left behind. The adventurous spirit of the adolescent remains, but without the emotional turmoil and desperate search for self-identity that belongs to that period of life.

When we connect with the divine presence waiting for us on the level below, we experience freedom from the limited ideas we had of God, and our spiritual journey blossoms again; we have reached a plateau, a whole new spiritual perspective. Of course, we get overattached to this place too, and so after a little respite, the Spirit suggests, "Let's look at the next level," and we are plunged into another transition or dark night.

What is most disconcerting for souls who have been on the journey for twenty or thirty years is that each time we make the transition from one level to the next, we are likely to encounter the same temptations we had before we started the journey, and we think, "I'm not getting anywhere; I'm just the same old stick." We may even think all is over or that we made a mistake to start the journey. Those commentaries are from our prerecorded memory bank and are just baloney.

What can we say about the distress that arises when the same old temptations recur? For example, difficulties with a particular person that we thought we had resolved once and for all recycle. In actual fact, it is not the same temptation at all. We encounter it again because there is a circular structure to a spiral staircase and hence horizontally we seem to meet the same old problem. But vertically we are now dealing with it at a more mature level. Hence, we are capable of making a more complete surrender of that attachment or that aversion. If the Spirit asked us in the beginning to make a total surrender of every difficult person or situation, nobody could do it. By leading us gradually (the way human things work), through growth in trust and humility, we are able to make an ever deeper surrender of ourselves to God. In this way we reach a new level of interior freedom, a deeper purity of heart, and an ever increasing union with the Spirit.

If God did not seem to disappear, how many of us would keep going? God is always one step ahead of us in this journey toward the center. Just as we think we have found him, he slips out of our grasp. The worst thing that can happen to us is to settle in an oasis under a palm tree. Growth is the challenge of the gospel. The great sin in the New Testament is to refuse to grow and to choose to stay as we are. The spiritual life is dynamic. The Spirit keeps inviting us to new levels of surrender, faith, and love.

The Divine Therapist continues the treatment in daily life. God brings people and events into our lives and takes them out again to show us other things we need to see about ourselves. Thus contemplative prayer and daily life work together if we are willing, and mutually reinforce the therapeutic process.

What happens when we come to the bottom of the spiral staircase and fully access the divine presence? It will be a great surprise and not like anything we expected. All the things we valued to reach that state will be seen in a new light and many former convictions may be shattered.

Every time we go down in this process (using the spiral model), we also move in the opposite direction by accessing a new level of freedom and growth in faith, hope, and charity under the influence of the Spirit (see Diagram 7). Every level down is also a level up and releases our creative energy. The humiliation of the false self leads to humility and humility leads to invincible trust. The fruits of the Spirit enumerated in Galatians 5:22–23 begin to appear and later the Beatitudes (Matt 5:3–10).

The transforming union seems to involve reappropriating every stage of our life, not with its details, but by reliving the values of each stage of life. We may realize that some of the things we rejected early in the spiritual journey were the result of misinformation. God invites us to take another look at the good things of life and its legitimate pleasures that we might have needlessly rejected. Everything good and of true value in life is reappropriated under the influence of the Spirit. It is as if we were led through our developmental process again, taking possession of the values appropriate to each level or period of life and letting go of the limitations that the human condition and our inability to handle them had imposed on us.

Will we ever come to the point where the false self and all the junk is emptied out? I think this is possible, but that does not mean that the results will be what we expected. On the contrary, the very capacity to love without self-interest is going to increase our capacity for suffering.

The journey, or process itself, is what Jesus called the Kingdom of God. This is a very important point. To accept our illness and whatever damage was done to us in life by people or circumstances is to participate in the cross of Christ and in our own redemption. In other words, the acceptance of our wounds is not only the beginning, but the journey itself. It does not matter if we do not finish it. If we are on the journey, we are in the Kingdom. This seems to be what Jesus is saying in the parables. It is in bearing our weakness with compassion, patience, and without expecting all our ills to go away that we function best in a Kingdom where the insignificant, the outcasts, and everyday life are the basic coordinates. The Kingdom is in our midst. Our attitude toward reality can go on improving as the Spirit — according to our personal history, determination, and all the other uncertain factors of life — enables us to negotiate the spiral staircase.

Rather than try to identify where we are on the spiral staircase or which dark night we are in, it is better to surrender to the process. The dark nights are helpful guides in a general way, but they take different forms in different people. For those living active lives in the world, external trials may predominate. For those living in solitude, interior trials seem to predominate. Both will certainly be present in some degree. For some people, the dark nights are very clear; for others, not so. Some people seem to be in them for longer periods than others, and some seem to be in and out of them or in both states at once.

Perfection, or holiness, it seems to me, should be measured by our commitment to the spiritual journey with its spiral staircase, rather than by attaining some particular goal. There are breakthroughs along the way, followed by plateaus in which we see our dark side as never before, but with growing serenity and acceptance. During these periods may also come experiences of divine union that then may take years to work into all our faculties, relationships, and bodies. But then the journey continues. We are called to a deeper humility, which in turn calls for a greater trust and an all-encompassing love of God. In a sense, the bottom and the top meet or collapse into one another. Humility and boundless confidence in God's infinite mercy merge, and the ongoing journey becomes whatever God wants it to be.

Chapter 9

The Deepening Experience of Centering Prayer

A S I HINTED IN THE LAST CHAPTER, I understand the un-conscious in a very different way from Freud while acknowledging the great contribution of his observational genius. In my terminology, which reflects a more Jungian viewpoint, the unconscious comprises both positive and negative elements. It contains within it potentials in our-selves that we are not yet aware of as well as emotional material and emotionally charged events that have been completely repressed.* Or to put it another way, we can distinguish two parts to the unconscious, one the *psycho-logical* and the other the *ontological* (level of being). The psychological contains our whole personal history, espe-cially emotional traumas, that we repressed at an early age, chiefly for survival motives.

The ontological unconscious, or level of being, contains all the human potentialities for spiritual development that have yet to be activated. These can be differentiated into the natural energies and the energies of grace. In a sense, both energies are divine since God is the creator and sus-tainer of both. The natural energies go by various names such as life force, dynamic ground, kundalini, cosmic en-ergy. Through them we participate in the creative process through which all things that exist emerge and to which they return. In Christian terms, it might be called "the

---

*The latter are to be distinguished from the subconscious, which is ma-terial that we deliberately place there and know it is there, like a mantra or aspiration that we have repeated so many times that it says itself — as, for example, the Jesus Prayer.

Light that enlightens everyone coming into the world" (prologue to the Gospel of John). This energy gradually unfolds, if it is not interfered with, from conception to full bodily maturity, and at the same time it serves through the brain and nervous system as the basis of mental and spiritual development.

Along with this innate and divinely created energy, which most of us are more or less out of touch with when we first set forth on the spiritual journey, there is the Divine Indwelling which Christians call the Father, Son, and Holy Spirit — three infinitely distinct "Persons" in one undivided unity, to use the terms of the early Fathers of the Church. This enormous but still unconscious divine life is bestowed on us in baptism, or with the desire for baptism expressed in a serious commitment to the spiritual journey. Thus, we share in the divine life, whether we know it or not, both by nature and by grace. The realization and actualization of this inherent human potential to be "divinized" — the term loved by the Greek Fathers of the Church — might be called the human adventure. The priority we give to this adventure determines more or less the extent of the ontological powers of the unconscious that will be actualized in our particular lives.

Because we are dealing with the unconscious, we sometimes run into blockages to our growth both human and divine. These may be physical, emotional, or spiritual. Centering Prayer, as it becomes contemplative in the strict sense, gently but relentlessly invites us to face up to issues that we are not acknowledging in our lives. Sometimes we do not even know what they are. Sometimes the problem is an unconscious process like one of the emotional programs for happiness, some aspects of which we have not yet recognized. The blockage alerts us to the fact that something in us is not giving way to God's will. But we seem to be powerless to do anything about it under our present circumstances. All we can do is wait and pray for the wall to fall down. And sometimes it is a long wait.

When we are doing Centering Prayer regularly (i.e., twice daily), there is a constant wearing away of our opposition to grace. There may be an unconscious resistance to acknowledging something God wishes to show us or to receiving something God wishes to give us. This resistance can manifest itself in different ways: for example, by physical symptoms like pain or a sense of not being able to say "yes" sincerely, or a generalized uneasiness. But if we can just wait it out and continue our regular practice of Centering Prayer, eventually the pocket of resistance begins to dissipate.

We normally come to full, reflective self-consciousness around the age of reason completely out of touch with the divine energy within us. Centering Prayer is the movement of consenting to God's presence and action within us. The longer we do the Centering Prayer practice, the less we may notice when we go to a deep place. So we think, "I'm not getting anywhere." We remember that there were times when we were strongly seized by the presence of God. The human organism has an incredible capacity to adjust to circumstances. People without an arm or a leg, who are blind, or who have some other physical disability, adjust to life. We can also get used to divine consolation or deep rest to such a degree that we do not even notice it. This does not mean that grace is any less active in us. We may have been absorbed in God often in the early days, but now after three or four years, our prayer time is like brushing our teeth; we just do it automatically every night and morning. If we experience the prayer of quiet, it does not make the same impression that it did when it was new. We sit and pray, but nothing seems to happen. We are aware of thoughts going by and then get up and go about our business, and day follows day.

In actual fact, the purifying process is going on all the time, but it no longer has the signposts it had when we could say, "Now I'm at rest, now I'm unloading, now I'm having primitive feelings, now I'm trying to return to the sacred word." The sense of rest is relative, so we have to deduce our deep absorption in God through other signs. One of these is the swift passage of time. We sit down and thoughts keep going by. Since we have not learned to ignore all prerecorded commentaries, the thought comes, "This isn't much of a prayer today." And yet as the beeper goes off at the end of our prayer period, it seems like we had just sat down. When we do not notice the passage of time or when it seems very short, we must have been in a deep place. Time is the measure of motion, of particular objects going by. When there are a lot of thoughts, prayer seems long. When we are aware of a lot of thoughts and prayer still seems like a short time, then we must have been firmly centered. Remember the great gospel teaching: the Kingdom of God is not in grandiose experiences, but in the passage of ordinary time. This is where the seeds of grace are growing. God intervenes in our prayer, but not so we would notice it. The deeper our prayer actually is, the more it habitually drops out of our ordinary awareness. When we experience spiritual consolation, this is our *interpretation* of the divine action within us. Hence it is conditioned by our cultural background, temperament, and personal history.

The subtler and more spiritual the experience of grace, the less we perceive it. This does not mean that we should resist spiritual experiences in the form of consolation, interior sweetness, or waves of love. We may need them. God speaks to us on every level of our consciousness at different times in our lives. But as we climb the ladder of consciousness beyond the rational level into the intuitive, our idea of God expands and God ceases to relate to us at the other levels.

Many contemplatives cannot do discursive meditation or make particular aspirations. They are just paralyzed. They can use these mental processes well enough outside the time of prayer, but as soon as they try to pray, they fall into a state of helplessness. The Spirit has taken over their prayer and she could not care less about their reflections.

Such acts are in fact only preliminaries to prayer. If the Spirit wants brilliant thoughts, she can call on the angels. If God was looking for geniuses, he would have created more of them. What God is after from humans, according to the Judeo-Christian tradition, is our love.

Thus deep rest can be present in prayer, but its source is on such a high frequency that it is no longer translated as rest or consolation. There is simply a mysterious attraction or hunger for God. This is one of the surest signs that one is progressing in contemplation. The Spirit moves us to renew our consent whenever it gets a little fuzzy because some flashy boat on the river of ordinary awareness conjures up one of the emotional programs with roots in the unconscious. Until we have completely emptied out the false self with its emotional programs for happiness along with their tormenting desires, passing thoughts will continue to cause aversions or attractions because there is still something to be stimulated in the unconscious. When there is no longer anything to stimulate, inner freedom is complete and peace is habitual.

The spiritual sense of rest that we experienced in the first few years begins to be refined into an abiding state that might be called "peace," a peace that is not sensible — i.e., perceptible to the senses. It is beyond joy and beyond sorrow because it is rooted in the divine presence. One is secure in the steadfast love of God. Our peace is subject to some alarms, however, as long as there is false self material that has not been evacuated and is thus susceptible to the stimulation that awakens the conscious or unconscious desires of one or other of our emotional programs.

Rest moves toward peace. Peace does not have a particular content. We are not peaceful *about* something. We are just peaceful. This is one place where the psalms are topnotch in explaining the experience: "I have calmed and quieted my soul. Like a child weaned on its mother's breast, so is my soul" (Ps 131). We see the image of the child whose fretful struggle for its mother's milk has finally subsided and who can accept mother as mother without bothering about her milk. Is this an advance or not?

If we can rest in God, not in the sense of a feeling, but in the sense of contentment with whatever the psychological content of our prayer may be, time goes fast. Once in a while we may uncover some unconscious material, but it is not dramatic anymore. Primitive emotions from early childhood may pop up, but after acute psychic nausea has been experienced a few times, we are no longer afraid of it. The newness of the experience is the reason why it may seem so traumatic at first. We go on unloading the undigested emotional material of a lifetime, but now the unloading of the unconscious tends to be relatively unobserved and to take place in the ordinary course of prayer.

This period is a passage from one level of consciousness or one level of faith to the next. The faith that worked through reason and the senses closes down after the springtime of the spiritual journey, especially in the recurring periods of the night of sense when the emotional programs for happiness are progressively uprooted by the divine action. Our own activity cannot heal us. Healing comes to us as we gradually submit to the divine action — including the time of weaning from the breasts of consolation — and accept in place of "felt" consolation the stable sense of God's presence on the level of pure faith. Pure faith does not seek rewards of any kind, especially sensible consolation, which might be called "spiritual junk food." The solid food of the spiritual journey is pure faith. It is the "narrow way that leads to life" and is exercised by waiting upon God in loving attentiveness without any specific psychological content.

Thus, intentionality is the star rising in the dark nights. It is the "focus" of contemplative prayer. As long as our intention remains pure — to serve God, to listen to God, to wait upon God, to surrender to God — then thoughts of whatever kind do not make any difference. They do not affect the purity of our prayer. In a sense we are what our will is doing. If our intention is firm to wait God out, submitting to the Divine Therapy, then the Divine Therapy is working.

Of course, our intention itself is not entirely beyond the reaches of the false self, even when the spiritual journey is well advanced. The false self is a master of delusion, and what we *think* we are doing for love of God and pure self-surrender can become subtly infected with spiritual pride. The final purgation of spiritual pride is traditionally known as the dark night of spirit. It is designed to free us from the residue of the false self in the unconscious and thus to prepare us for transforming union. Until this final purgation is undergone, we do the best we can with our intentionality, acknowledging and renouncing our subtle attachments as soon as they are perceived. We can bring the false self to liturgy and to the reception of the sacraments, but we cannot bring the false self forever to contemplative prayer because it is the nature of contemplative prayer to dissolve it.

The higher the frequency on which God communicates with us, the greater the divine transmission. There are no faculties to interpret the highest level. Faith alone contacts it. How? By our consent. Nothing could be easier. At first it is hard to be content with this radical simplicity. How can we miss God if God is totally present? That is the problem. All spiritual exercises are designed to reduce the monumental illusion that God is absent. Not so. We just think so. Since the way we think is the way we usually act, we live as if God were absent. Whatever we can do to contribute to the dissolution of that confusion furthers our spiritual journey.

The unloading of the unconscious usually takes the form of emotionally charged thoughts. When our prayer settles down, the unloading becomes less obvious, except during a particular period of purification like an intense period in one of the dark nights. It should be obvious from Diagram 5 (page 77) that thoughts and rest are two moments in the same circular process. By resisting thoughts or by treating them as distractions, we are also resisting the unloading process and thus delaying our healing. If we don't resist, the process goes on. Thus the primary practice is just doing it.

Of course, we have a right to know whether Centering Prayer is good for us. But we can only test that assumption by its effects in daily life. And what are those effects? There is something in human nature that equates success with something big. But this is not God's value system. By returning to the sacred word again and again, we gradually are wearing away the layers of false self until they are emptied out. Then our intention is not challenged anymore. It is always just "Yes." Our behavior becomes more and more motivated by divine love, which is totally self-giving, rather than by the self-centered universe or homemade self that we created in childhood in order to survive.

One other phenomenon needs to be pointed out here for the sake of those who are experienced in this practice. By "experienced" I mean those who have been doing it regularly, twice a day, year after year. Suppose you start your prayer and are moving into rest or peace. To beginners we say, "Whenever you notice you are thinking about some other thought, return ever-so-gently to the sacred word." Later we say, "Return to the sacred word whenever you notice you are *attracted* to some other thought." A beginner might not be able to grasp that distinction.

The sacred word is an intention, a movement of the will toward the spiritual level of our being. As we access peace, a double level of awareness may appear. Let us suppose that thoughts are going by, such as something that happened twenty-five years ago, what is going to happen tomorrow, or maybe a plan about next summer's vacation. At the same time we know that we are not interested in these thoughts. We think, "Should I go back to the sacred word?" The very fact that we can think, "Should I go back to the sacred word?" means that we should *not* go back, because we are already where the sacred word is facilitating us to go. The sacred word cannot do more than that. If we are in a place of peace, we do not need our usual method because to abide in deep peace *is* the method.

Sometimes in Centering Prayer we experience two levels of consciousness at the same time: the awareness of thoughts and feeling — perceptions we are not interested in — and the awareness of a presence, however delicate, that we are committed to and experiencing, however subtly. In this case, no matter how many thoughts go by, we pay no attention. It is like noise in the street or music at the supermarket. We ignore it and simply put up with it. If we try to return to the sacred word to get rid of the noise, we are needlessly disturbing our peace. It is only when we notice an attractive thought that starts to pull us back to ordinary awareness (the surface of the river) that we need to return to the sacred word. Moreover, since we are in a place that is very refined, we do not have to say the sacred word clearly. We can just take note that it is absent or start to say it. That may be enough to restore the movement toward interior peace. But we have to do something, however delicate, to maintain the purity of our intention when it is challenged.

In a period of heavy unloading, what is coming from the unconscious is like a subterranean volcano erupting or an earthquake. Or we feel a tidal wave of thoughts, perceptions, and emotions that bury the sacred word. We cannot find it or if we do, it is of no help. In this case, the acceptance of the situation just as it is can be our sacred symbol for the time being. In other words, the *fact* of the primitive emotions or distressing thoughts in our awareness can be the symbol of our intention to be with God. When they subside, we return to the sacred word once again as if nothing had happened. It was just a squall. Even if we have been in a hurricane, we do not think about it. We are simply happy it is over and return to the sacred word.

Peace is the right relationship to everything: God, ourselves, other people, the cosmos. It is a balancing act. The experience of it is so subtle that we may think it is no experience. It *is* an experience, but if we are expecting something more, we think it is nothing. It is like the mustard seed in the gospel parable. It looks ever so small, but leave it alone and it will grow into a bush. We must keep our sights within the realm of the ordinary because that is where the Kingdom of God really is. If we get out of the realm of the ordinary, we have to ask if this is really the Kingdom. I am more worried about great experiences, especially visions and locutions, than I would be about unloading the unconscious. The former are much harder to deal with. It is hard to believe that they are not communications directly from God, but in actual fact, they are only our interpretation of these communications.

The most safe, secure, comprehensive reception of God, according to John of the Cross, is pure faith. It is in his words "the proximate means to divine union." A wonderful teaching, very pure, but it does not hold out any hope for the desire for compensatory satisfaction. Such desires slow down its coming. The desire for compensation, when translated into the spiritual journey, reaches out for spiritual goodies and junk food. God has to purify all that stuff out.

What, then, is the real food, and how does it nourish us? The author of Hebrews distinguishes body, soul, and spirit as the three basic elements of a human being. The physical body is the historical body that we are living in. The soul possesses its own special kind of energy. One of its manifestations is our emotions, as we experience them in relationships with others. For example, we feel compassion or instant rapport with someone. The other person may not have said anything. We may not know a thing about the person's life or aspirations, but something inside resonates with this person, and we know that we want to be friends. Or someone might say to us, "What you did touched me deeply." We did not actually touch this person at all, but there was an emotional interaction.

"Spirit" presumably refers to our spiritual energies, which is simply another way of describing the Holy Spirit's presence and action in our lives. As we saw in Diagrams 3 and 4 (pages 62 and 67), underlying our ordinary level of psychological awareness is a deeper level of spiritual awareness where we are intimately attuned to God at a more subtle level than our ordinary faculties of thinking and feeling. It is to this level that Centering Prayer addresses itself. Even more intimate is the awareness of the Divine Indwelling at the core of our being. When these spiritual energies are activated (which is a matter of our becoming increasingly sensitive to them, since God is never absent) and we are in actual contact with their full potentialities, the less we perceive them on the lower levels. Sensible consolation and reflection drop away. They are still available, but our way of relating to God is no longer dependent on them.

God seems to nourish us at each of these levels — body, soul, and spirit. As our personal development progresses, our idea of God becomes more expanded and profound. The Spirit reorders all the disorders that we experience in ourselves so that we can express the divine energy appropriately on each level of our being.

According to quantum physics, various levels of material energy can occupy the same physical space at the same time. In similar fashion, the divine energy can be at work in us at levels that cannot be perceived at all. That does not mean they are not real or present. On the level of grace, faith is purified of attachments and excessive dependency on ways that are good as stepping stones, but inadequate to manifest the full range of the divine presence and action. The spiritual journey as such may drop out of our immediate awareness. The divine energy is most powerful when it is least perceived by our faculties. When we sit down to do Centering Prayer and form our intention, we know the divine presence is already there. We do not create it. All we have to do is consent. The divine energy flows into us and through us. In its purest form it is available twenty-four hours a day at maximum strength. By consenting, we open to God as God is without trying to figure who or what God is. We consent to the divine presence without depending on a medium to express it, translate it, or interpret it in terms of our personal history, cultural conditioning, and temperamental bias. God communicates himself on only one condition. Our consent. Visions, consolations, experiences, psychological breakthroughs, all have value but only a limited value, pointing us to the maximum value, which is the whole of God in pure faith. This faith, once it is established as a conviction, changes our perspective of who we are and who God is. It operates appropriately through the theological virtues and the Seven Gifts of the Spirit, enabling us to respond to the realities and routines of daily life and to perceive the divine presence in the ordinary, the insignificant, and even in suffering.

There remains a further energy, which is reserved for the next life. That is what theologians call the Beatific Vision. This requires freedom from the limitations of the physical body in order to experience it. This energy is so intense that if it were not mediated by the ordinary affairs of daily life that distract us from continual contact with the divine energy, we would turn into a grease spot. This is the energy that lights the universe and forms the whirling nebulae. We can receive only a little of it at a time. In heaven we can have all we want. We can sink our teeth, so to speak, into the divine essence, because then our bodies will be glorified and able to handle that energy.

Chapter 10

The Spiritual Direction of Contemplatives

I DO NOT BELIEVE that one can become a spiritual director just by taking an academic course, however useful
this might be as a conceptual background for offering spiritual counsel. Similarly, a psychological background can be
very useful, but it is primarily intended to make one a good
psychological counselor. It does not automatically produce
someone who can discern the delicate movements of the
Spirit in people coming for spiritual direction.

Centering Prayer, as we have already seen, is a particular method of preparing for contemplative prayer. Those
following this path need a director who has personal
knowledge and experience of this path. Sometimes spiritual directors or retreat directors trained in the literature of
the Christian contemplative tradition think they can teach
Centering Prayer after reading a few books on the subject.
However, to teach Centering Prayer requires special training and a long period of its regular practice, without which
we do not fully understand its subtleties and hence cannot impart it adequately to other people. Since Centering
Prayer is a receptive method, the psychological effects of
such a method need to be foreseen by the director. The dark
nights may start fairly soon in such a practice, and then the
director needs to be a good listener and know how to give
plenty of reassurance. A Centering Prayer support group
that has been meeting for some time can often provide this
kind of encouragement better than a director, particularly
one who has little or no experience of the dark nights.

In general, the direction of contemplatives requires

some special sensitivities. One of these is a particular alertness to maintaining a balance of inner and outer activities. A purely apophatic prayer may stagnate without some conceptual input through spiritual reading, liturgy, or listening to sermons or lectures that speak to the contemplative person's state of prayer. There needs to be a balance of intellectual, affective, and intuitive elements in prayer. Contemplative prayer frees us from *attachment* to the use of our faculties in going to God, not from their use. The right use of them disposes us for the gifts of wisdom, understanding, and knowledge, which lead to contemplative prayer in the full sense of the term.

Centering Prayer is a further dimension of relating to Christ, a relationship developed in reflection and affective prayer but moving beyond it. It is "resting in God," to quote St. Gregory the Great. But one is not forever resting even if one's prayer is restful. There must be action, prompted by the attitude of faith and love accessed in times of resting in God. The resting of Centering Prayer has to be manifested in daily life. Otherwise any prayer, especially if it is consoling or peaceful, can degenerate into a high-class tranquilizer, leaving us in the same situation we were in before, namely, of attachment to self-centered goals or preoccupations and insensitivity to the needs of other people. Thus the interaction between daily life and prayer assimilates us to the contemplative dimension of the gospel, which demands not just prayer alone or good deeds alone.

Christ is always the teacher. The transmission of his experience of God as Abba, loving Father, is the work of contemplative prayer, to which all spiritual guidance is in service. Thus for Christians, the liturgy celebrated in the Christian assembly, especially the Eucharist, is an essential part of the Divine Therapy since it is the transmission of the graces attached to the major events of Christ's life. Contemplative prayer will deepen one's appreciation of the liturgy and one's capacity to receive the divine transmission present in the Christian assembly and especially in the sacraments. The better prepared we are through contemplative prayer and action, the more profoundly will the presence of Christ in the Christian assembly reach into the depths of our being and transform us at every level. Without this grounding in a full Christian life, contemplative prayer can take us only part of the way toward the transforming union.

In earlier chapters I have tried to develop a conceptual background for the experience of the spiritual journey, using the "Divine Therapy" as a paradigm. This paradigm can be useful for those who are also called to be spiritual directors. There will be times when contemplatives feel they cannot pray anymore. All that is left to them is the desire to pray, sometimes buried under enormous difficulties in daily life along with interior purification. They need to be reminded again and again that the desire to pray is itself a prayer. St. John of the Cross wrote with great insight, "Love consists not in feeling great things, but in having great detachment and in suffering for the Beloved." The love of God is not a question of feeling but of choice, and this choice is put to the test during the transitional periods on the spiral staircase that St. John of the Cross calls the dark night. Thus someone who wants to pray *is* praying, and someone who feels no love *is* loving as long as he or she continues to remain available both in prayer and in daily life to the Divine Therapist. Trust in God has to be proposed vigorously and without end to those who are struggling on the spiritual journey with prolonged periods of powerlessness, dryness, and even the sense of being abandoned by God. These are signs of progress, not regression.

At times, the loss of the presence of God can cause such deep mourning we may think that someone we are trying to help is in a depression. We have to distinguish clearly a clinical depression from depressed feelings. The latter are the natural and inevitable consequence of the sense of loss in someone who has been experiencing sensible consolation and is now struggling with a lack of apparent benefit, profit, or any feeling of love toward Christ.

What distinguishes the dark night from a depression is the fact that a person in the dark night normally has an intuition that these trials are going someplace. One perceives at times the fruits of the dark night in one's changing perspectives such as the growth of a nonjudgmental attitude toward everyone, greater detachment from things and persons, humility, and trust in God. In a clinical depression one goes around in circles getting nowhere and can perceive no benefit at all on any level. In some persons both mental states can be present at once. In this case, the person should get psychological help for the depression. One who is simply in the dark night should not be given pills or tranquilizers indiscriminately. They may interfere with the process of grace. This particular area of discernment is sometimes a close judgment call.

Another fairly reliable indicator that should be mentioned here is the level of normal functioning. Those in the dark night, though they may be feeling inwardly that their world has collapsed, will generally continue to function in their job and relationships. The general disposition of acceptance of God's will contrasts markedly with the self-preoccupation, at times severe, of clinical depression, which often brings function in the world to a standstill.

As the foregoing example suggests, the method of Centering Prayer involves a good deal of interface with psychology; in fact, it was specifically developed as a dialogue between contemporary psychological models and the classic language of the Christian spiritual path. In the model of Centering Prayer, the heart of Christian purification lies in the struggle with unconscious motivations, and the prayer itself encourages the emergence of previously unconscious material. Thus, the spiritual director needs to be prepared for what emerges — not to assume the role of psychotherapist oneself, but to offer encouragement while recognizing when additional expertise may be called for.

Gerald May, a clinical psychologist and co-founder of the Shalem Institute for Spiritual Direction, distinguishes very well between psychological counseling, pastoral counseling, and spiritual direction. Although these overlap in some degree, each one has a particular emphasis and an integrity that needs to be respected. Thus, there needs to be close cooperation between psychology and spiritual direction. Neurotic and even psychotic symptoms can arise in the course of the spiritual journey, and in some cases there has to be referral for psychological help. This does not mean that the spiritual journey has come to an end for these people. It simply means that special care and treatment may be needed because of emotional damage surfacing in the course of spiritual development. One's capacity to face the dark side of one's personality increases in direct proportion as one's trust in God develops, and even more when one experiences oneself as loved by God. All the defenses disintegrate in the presence of knowing one is loved by God.

When difficulties arise, the directee normally needs to be encouraged to persevere in the practice, not to shop around for another method. Centering Prayer has the great benefit of providing an established framework in which the night of sense takes place with fewer traumatic side effects because one is accustomed to letting go of thoughts and feelings as basic to the practice. A spiritual director experienced in Centering Prayer will not be "spooked" by the impression that the directee is getting worse instead of better and can offer the crucially needed encouragement to relax and trust the process.

Only very occasionally are there danger signs, and almost always these are the result of an underlying emotional fragility or of a willfulness motivated by the false self coopting the process and pushing too hard. The psyche has a tremendous capacity for health and normally will not unload more than a person is psychologically ready to face. If unloading happens too fast, prayer can be cut back, but only when there is serious depression or pre-psychotic symptoms should the prayer be eliminated altogether. Twenty to thirty minutes twice a day seems to be the normal time span to enable the prayer to do its work. More than three hours a day generally requires supervision by an experienced guide or the format of Centering Prayer Intensive Retreats. The same format should not be continued as a regular practice once back at home.

A spiritual director needs to be aware of the dynamics of his or her own personality with its dark side and its special needs. Many people go into psychological counseling in order to know more about their own needs or to distract themselves from them. In the psychological relationship, just as in prayer, two things are involved: the development of bonding, rapport, and friendship with the therapist, and the healing or treatment that is required in order to restore health to the whole person. Excessive or misdirected friendship can get in the way of the healing. Or the treatment may be too harsh. Hence the delicate balance that is required in the spiritual direction of contemplatives. If our own psychological dynamics are at work, or if we have our own unfulfilled emotional needs, then our spiritual direction may become possessive or we can become too emotionally involved. This is manifested when we feel hurt when someone we are directing decides to go to someone else. Feelings of jealousy or envy are a sure sign of attachment. Emotional overinvolvement is also a sure sign that it is time to back off or get psychological help ourselves. At times the overinvolvement can lead to sexual feelings toward the person that we are trying to help. Or a youthful person who comes to us for direction can become the son or daughter that we never had.

On the side of the directee, transference can become dependency if at some point the spiritual director does not insist on the directee's taking personal responsibility for himself or herself. The director has to respect the spiritual integrity of the directee and not lay any trips — emotional, intellectual, or disciplinary — on that person. The encouragement of personal responsibility is essential. The other person should always feel free to leave the relationship.

As spiritual directors, we need to pay attention to our own spiritual nurturing. We ourselves have to be qualified by faithful practice of contemplative prayer and by taking the time to remain authentic and to grow by means of regular retreat days and yearly retreats to deepen our own experience of the path. The deeper our experience of the path, the more we will be able to support others on theirs.

A word about people who have been deeply involved in another tradition and who want to teach Centering Prayer. This seems to be a natural consequence of their previous experience. Not a few persons who have deeply involved themselves in an Eastern tradition have felt a desire to return to their roots, especially if they were raised as Christians. The need for a personal aspect in their relationship with God opens up as their Eastern practice quiets their emotions and lays to rest any indignation they may have had toward their early Christian training. Even though these people are often very capable and are good teachers in the sense of having extensive practical experience in Eastern meditation, they need to take plenty of time to reassimilate the conceptual background of Christian prayer and study the tradition in depth. Otherwise, without realizing it, they may insinuate a number of principles or attitudes from the previous tradition in which they were deeply involved and mix in elements of their previous meditative methods rather than teach the integrity of the Centering Prayer method. They should work with someone else who has a lot of experience before setting out on their own.

To sum up, spiritual direction should address itself to where each person is. Beginners on the journey need concrete instruction as regards the regular practice of prayer, a simple rule of life, and suggested readings. For those who are established in a prayer practice, there is need for Lectio

Divina and study as well as practice for daily life. Several appropriate practices are suggested in the final chapter of my book *Invitation to Love* (Element, 1992). In general, their goal is to encourage the contemplative attitudes of consent and a prompt letting go of afflictive emotions arising in daily life. And of course, encouragement becomes essential as the dark night unfolds.

For those who are more advanced on the spiritual journey, the support of friendship and understanding is the greatest gift one can offer. One can usually help in the measure of one's own experience of the dark nights and passive purification. The encouragement and reassurance of one who has been over the same path and the validation of one's own experience as coming from God that only an experienced spiritual director can give are enormous gifts. The best direction aims at enabling or empowering the directee to graduate to the more refined and delicate guidance of the Spirit in all matters. The director becomes a fellow traveler and friend on the journey, and the directee and director speak the truth to each other in love. Speaking just the truth can be too harsh. Speaking the truth in love is mutually sustaining.

Chapter 11

A Contemplative Vision for Our Times

Adapted from a talk originally given to the National Faculty of Contemplative Outreach, Ltd., at its annual meeting at Chrysalis House, Warwick, N.Y., January 1993.

I ENVISIONED CONTEMPLATIVE OUTREACH as an experiment to see if the fruit of the contemplative experience that I received in a Cistercian monastery could be made available to people who want to lead a life of prayer outside a monastic context. It was not with a view to forming a community that we started offering Centering Prayer retreats at Spencer back in the late 1970s. Rather we began in the usual way that retreats have been given for centuries. A preacher is selected, gives a few excellent lectures, and then nobody ever sees him again. Next year the community chooses another retreat master.

My conviction grew that we could not introduce the contemplative life for people without some ongoing formation or support system. Actually that was the original purpose of primitive monastic life, whether it was conscious or not. The idea of the first monastics was, "Let's get out of this noisy world, this corrupt Roman civilization, and find the best possible milieu in which we can be quiet with the Lord and develop both our prayer and the ascetic life." So following the inspiration of the great St. Anthony of Egypt, thousands of people headed into the deserts of Egypt and Palestine. They figured if he did it, they could do it too. Thus, the monastic lifestyle began. As a lifestyle it was directed entirely toward the developing of the contemplative dimension of the gospel. The first monastics understood their vocation as the following of Christ in a comprehensive way that involved both deep prayer and the practice of asceticism. The two were embraced together.

Observing the great influx of Eastern masters and the great attraction they had for people in the 1960s and 1970s, a few of us at St. Joseph's Abbey, in Spencer, Massachusetts, started asking ourselves whether it would be possible to put our own contemplative monastic tradition into a form that ordinary people could understand and practice. Encouraged by the Second Vatican Council, which had urged the Church to try to express theology and Christian doctrine in modern terms and contemporary language, it seemed to us that something similar should be done for the contemplative tradition of the Church. It was then that Fr. William Meninger worked out a "how-to" method that was aimed at expressing the richness of *The Cloud of Unknowing*, an anonymous fourteenth-century classic, in a form that would make it accessible to people in our day. Without some how-to method of contemplatively oriented prayer, people were being attracted in great numbers to the well-thought-out and well-presented methods of Eastern masters who were arriving in increasing numbers in this country. This search for a spiritual dimension to life was no passing fancy in those days. Though thousands were going to India every summer in search of spirituality and a guru, very few of them thought of inquiring at a Benedictine or Cistercian monastery about whether they could find a form of spirituality there. The Christian contemplative tradition was believed to be locked up in cloisters. Even there, it often existed in a truncated form with an overemphasis on monastic observances rather than on interior transformation. I felt that the situation cried out for some response from contemplative monks and nuns. Although we started off in the early 1970s imagining that our method would be of interest to clergy and those in religious orders, we did not envisage that it would be of much interest to lay people. They had been thoroughly convinced by their Catholic education that any aspiration for contemplative prayer could be realized only in a cloister. What an irony that the original movement toward contemplative prayer, which had come from lay people looking for a structure to support their spiritual aspirations, had wound up over the centuries as the exclusive preserve of an institution. The unquestioned assumption was that contemplation could not be found anywhere except in a cloister, if indeed it could be found there.

This has left us in our time without a sense of the immense possibility that the gospel opens out to lay persons and indeed almost commands them to pursue. Evelyn Underhill is one of the outstanding writers on mysticism of our era. She offers a parable of the spiritual journey that might be apropos here. She wrote that the spiritual journey is like the migration of English sparrows, each weighing about an ounce and a quarter, who twice each year take off into the unknown, committing themselves to the air and flying over the ocean where there are no landmarks to give them any guidance. And yet without any hesitation, every fall thousands of them take off, and in the spring thousands return undergoing the same hazards. This migration, she claims, is a good example of what the spiritual journey is all about. We have no idea of where we are going. There are all kinds of difficulties we cannot foresee. The birds commit themselves to the elements by way of blind trust in their instinct. The spiritual journey is basically a surrender in blind trust to our conviction that what we hope to find on the journey we either already have or will certainly find. But there is no guarantee that we will arrive safely on the basis of the evidence or our circumstances. We must let go and let the wind (the Holy Spirit) take us where we hope to go.

One of the reasons why contemplatives have always been in the minority in this world is because contemplation involves a surrender of one's whole self, not just a period of time set aside each day for some form of prayer or meditation. It is a commitment of immense proportions and requires an eminent trust that God will bring us where we hope to go if we submit to this inner conviction or urging that we have to start. It does not matter how many difficulties there are, we have to go. There is no turning back once we have started because the sky is a big place, and we had better stay with the flock. The image of these little English sparrows fighting storms and winds to get to their destination is a moving symbol of our own situation. In our case, however, taking to the air is not based on instinct, but rather on the theological virtue of hope. The movement, call, or attraction that God has given us is a promise that is just as reliable as the instinct of the birds as they surrender to their migratory instinct. Instead of surrendering to a migratory instinct, we surrender to God's transforming process.

In the early days of teaching Centering Prayer, I perceived that people had to have some kind of adequate support system if they were going to persevere in the practice. One of the great supports of migration, I suppose, is flying in flocks. A dangerous and long journey to nowhere needs company.

Naturally a lot of initial enthusiasts lose interest when they get the message that Centering Prayer is not a shortcut to bliss. At best, it may provide a few months of peace before the real trials and difficulties begin. Recently someone did a thesis on Centering Prayer along with several forms of Eastern meditation, recommending them as means to lessen anxiety. It was found (but based on too small a selection of people to be convincing) that meditation in general, including Centering Prayer, reduces anxiety. I wrote to this man, "Centering Prayer will reduce anxiety perhaps for the first three months. But once the unconscious starts to unload, it will give you more anxiety than you ever had in your life." The spiritual journey requires dedication; hence, some people are going to back out. It involves a commitment of the whole person — body, soul, and spirit. Centering Prayer is totally in the service of sustaining us in a transforming process which is anything but secure,

easy, or certain. The theological virtue of hope is the antic-
ipation of the end, here and now. According to Jesus, we
already have eternal life if we believe in him. We just have
not realized it yet because we have not completed the flight.

The vision of Contemplative Outreach is this: "How can
we serve the Church and the broader Christian community, by making the rich Christian contemplative tradition
available in our day with the kind of language, inspiration,
and support system that will enable contemporary people to pursue the journey to the end?" In developing this
support system, I turned for a conceptual background to
certain psychological paradigms because I think that very
few seekers are going to start the spiritual journey today by
reading the spiritual classics. I wonder if any would have
started Centering Prayer if I had not put it into a psychological frame of reference that they could identify with. I
don't think the study of the old classics is the way to start.
How many people can extrapolate a practical method of
prayer from reading two or three hundred spiritual classics, most of them with a very different vocabulary and
reference points from our own? The Christian tradition has
always been somewhat limited in methodology. There is a
lot of excellent material on original sin and the Fall and the
terrible state we are in as a result of the seven capital sins.
There is also quite a bit of exuberant literature on the transforming union and its joys, but there is not much that says
how you get from one place to the other.

This is where I received some inspiration from the East.
The Eastern masters began arriving in America in great
numbers after World War II saying, "Here is our method of
contemplative prayer [they called it meditation]. Where is
yours?" To which we had virtually nothing to reply. We did
not have any kind of method comparable to their concrete
and detailed instructions. Even the Spiritual Exercises of
St. Ignatius were in a pretty sorry state in those days, offering various useful visualizations, good in themselves, but
in no way capable of moving one to the more refined lev-

els of faith or to the contemplative state. The Jesuits have done much in recent decades to recover Ignatius's original inspiration and method. Centering Prayer was developed to offer Christians access to the richness of our own contemplative tradition. And by the early 1980s, it was clear that this method was going to meet a very real hunger. People were responding in increasing numbers and their lives as well as their prayer were being transformed.

Anyone who does any kind of serious prayer practice needs to have a conceptual background to deepen and integrate the practice. I knew that this need would be in great demand rather soon if people kept doing Centering Prayer. In working up the material that eventually became the Spiritual Journey video tape series, I tried to bring the Christian contemplative tradition into dialogue with contemporary science, especially developmental psychology, anthropology, and physics. I did not expect at first that anybody would be interested in it — certainly not lay persons. But I soon found out that lay persons were much more interested than the average priest or religious. I also became aware that people of other Christian denominations were interested too because they did not have a contemplative focus in their own denomination and were beginning to feel the need of something more experiential than sermons and theology. Even some priests and bishops were beginning to question whether the way to reconvert or evangelize people was to start with the liturgy or with catechetical instruction. Some kind of prayer experience looked like a more promising way to begin, something that would get people out of their heads.

The term "meditation" means for people exposed to Eastern methods what we Christians mean by contemplation, that is, a way of disregarding the usual flow of thoughts for a certain period of time. From a physiological/psychological point of view, that is really the essence of any form of Eastern meditation. As Carlos Castañeda put it in a classic phrase, "Stop the interior dialogue." That is a most useful discipline to prepare the mind for contemplative prayer. The process of committing oneself to the divine guidance is not a "hands-on" feeling; quite the contrary, it is the courage to proceed without any divine "hands-on," that is, to move into the dark nights where the real journey takes place and without which one does not normally reach the Promised Land.

Our organization is definitely not a form of lay monastic life. I deliberately rejected that paradigm because I knew as soon as we used the term "monastic," the average citizen would be back into the institutionalized view of contemplation, which is for cloistered people only. Most secular priests have the same concept. I remember a priest saying that in the seminary he attended, when the professor of spiritual theology came to the place where the text referred to contemplation, he said, "We won't go into that stuff here. That's for the boys up at Spencer." As if contemplation had nothing to do with persons in the active ministry! That was the universal mind-set we were dealing with until around 1975. One could not talk about contemplation even to cloistered people without some getting up and leaving or with most becoming very nervous. The rank and file were taught that contemplation is only for mystics and saints. In actual fact, contemplation is not the reward of a virtuous life; it is a *necessity* for a virtuous life. We will be waiting a long time for priests, and for the lay people who are now assuming many of the duties of priests, to be capable of spiritual guidance. It cannot be looked upon as just another of their many professional competencies. They have to be touched or enlightened by the fact that we do not make ourselves spiritual directors but commit, submit, and surrender ourselves to the journey without the props we would like to have to feel secure. In fact, the letting go of security is something we have to agree to as a condition for the journey. Without having accepted the trip into the unknown, one is really not a candidate for contemplation because that is what is presupposed. God has to lead us into a place that involves a complete reversal of our prepackaged values, a complete undoing of all our carefully laid plans, and a lot of letting go of our preconceived ideas.

Motivation is everything in the spiritual journey. God, I think, cares less about a change of lifestyle or ideal circumstances than about our attitude toward what we are doing. Our motivation can be inspired by the false self system dressed up in religious or spiritual garb. This letting go into the unknown, this submitting to the unloading process, is an essential step into the mystery of our own unconscious. Hidden there is not only our whole life's history, especially the emotional wounds of early childhood buried in the warehouse of our bodies, but also the positive elements of our potential for growth in faith, hope, and divine love, and where the Divine Indwelling is also present. We must gradually recover the conviction, not just the feeling, of the Divine Indwelling, the realization that God — Father, Son, and Holy Spirit — is living in us. This is the heart of the spiritual journey, to which Centering Prayer is totally in service.

I am often asked to clarify the relationship between Centering Prayer and Lectio Divina. Centering Prayer is not a part of the method of Lectio Divina. It is rather a distinct method of prayer that emerges out of the same tradition. It is closely related to Lectio Divina, but not so much in its method as in the developing relationship with Christ that Lectio Divina implies and fosters.

One of the practical consequences of Centering Prayer is overcoming the obstacles to the full development of Lectio Divina in our time because people are enculturated to oppose its spontaneous movement toward contemplative prayer. Some people have bright minds and are intellectually geared to endless reflection. This is not to say that some reflection on the truths of faith is not necessary. The problem with Lectio is how to get from simplified affective prayer to contemplation? I became increasingly convinced that Centering Prayer or some such method was normally necessary for people of our time to reach contemplation through the practice of Lectio.

In our time there is a predominant enculturation in the two things that are most inimical to proceeding from discursive meditation to interior silence. The first is hyperactivity — thinking that we have to *do* something in prayer to please God. The second is overconceptualization, a special hazard for those who are highly educated, and even more so for those who are highly trained theologically. They have gradually absorbed the idea that thinking about God is praying. It isn't. Centering Prayer is a way of enabling people of our time to get over these two major cultural obstacles to their development in prayer. In Lectio we are supposed to reflect, respond, and then in some mysterious fashion rest in God.

There is no common teaching in our time as to how one moves from discursive meditation to resting in God. In fact, until very recently this movement was specifically discouraged. For centuries in Jesuit communities for fear of a privatized mysticism one had to stick to discursive meditation. The historical result of this mentality is not surprising: contemplation became institutionalized and hence available only in certain highly structured circumstances, which were not remotely accessible to lay persons or even to those in the active ministry, not to mention busy monks and nuns in cloisters. But without the experience of resting in God, all the capital sins can flourish without one actually being aware of the fact. One may think one is doing great things for God if one gets into parochial work or teaching, but the seven capital sins, the results of the emotional programs for happiness in the unconscious, are there in concrete form and, unless confronted, will lead to burn-out or pharisaism, the occupational hazards of religious people.

This is the reason why I say one can't do the spiritual life nowadays without some working knowledge of one's own psychology. Unless one develops a healthy self-identity, the psychological resources for the journey are lacking. People who have been injured in early childhood and do not have a strong ego because they were oppressed or abused do not have a self to give to God. They do not have a self to relate either to God or to anybody else. When they hear advice like "humble yourself," or "keep your eyes always cast down," or "never question authority," they fall right into step because that is what they really like to do. They don't want to take responsibility for themselves and the damage that was done to them in early life. They prefer external obedience to inner transformation. But without personal responsibility for our emotional life, however wounded it is, the journey will never really get off the ground. Our conscious life has to be our starting point, of course, but the biggest problem is our unconscious motivation. Both have to be changed.

Centering Prayer creates the atmosphere in which that change can begin to take place. Some people will perceive that this practice is going to cause changes in them and back off. People who are prepsychotic and in a depression should do it only under professional guidance because Centering Prayer makes one vulnerable to the unconscious. One needs to have a sufficiently strong ego or self-identity to be able to deal with painful emotional material when it comes up.

A trip into the unconscious is a passage into the great unknown. One of the reasons we recommend limiting Centering Prayer to two periods a day is that with such a gentle exposure to the unconscious, the passage will take several years, unless some previous form of deep meditation has loosened up some stuff that might surface fairly soon. Apart from the latter consideration, people normally have plenty of time to grasp the conceptual background of the practice so that when the unconscious begins to unload and they get in touch with childhood traumas and instinctual drives, they will have the capacity to handle them. The experience will still be painful, but it will not blow them away.

To emphasize a most important point: *Centering Prayer is both a relationship and a method to foster that relationship at the same time.* It is tucked into the relational dynamic of Lectio Divina, although we can't exactly affirm that it is a part of Lectio or that it emerges from Lectio. It is also a method designed to reduce the obstacles to contemplation, especially overactivity, overdependence on one's thought, and excessive preoccupation with oneself and one's acts. The method itself is a discipline to enable the developing relationship with Jesus to reach its term in union with God. You have only to talk to people whose prayer is basically visualization or discursive meditation to realize you are on a different plane. No one understands contemplative prayer without some experience of it.

Centering Prayer relates to Lectio Divina as a discipline designed to correct what hinders or prevents us from moving from simplified affective prayer into contemplation. This does not mean that if we practice Centering Prayer, we never do anything else. We simply do Lectio and other forms of prayer at another time.

Now the delicate question arises, Can we *begin* a life of prayer with Centering Prayer? Tradition says that we should normally begin with discursive meditation and that we should not move beyond affective prayer unless we know God is calling us to contemplation. But nobody explains what that really means, or how we are to know when God is calling us. The usual signs given by St. John of the Cross are not easy to verify in concrete cases. We may go to a spiritual director who is supposed to help us discern, but he or she really may not know either. My question is why do we need to know?

Let us take another look at the continuum in Diagram 1 (page 56). The action of the Holy Spirit is directed toward us from one end and our efforts to pray are directed or open to the Spirit from the other end. According to the Roman Catholic faith, we cannot even desire to pray without the grace of the Holy Spirit. In this sense, every prayer is inspired by the Spirit. We say that the Spirit gradually takes over our prayer and that Centering Prayer is in the service of that project. But remember, "gradually" is our category, not God's. Conversion, or metanoia, is always presented in Scripture as a unified action, a recognition that stops us dead in our tracks and turns our lives in a different direction. If, under the prompting of the Spirit, a chronic alcoholic can realize that his life is unmanageable and turn it over to God, why is it so hard to imagine a person, even an "inexperienced" Christian, being moved by the contemplative gifts of wisdom, understanding, and knowledge while praying? It is not that hard for God.

To return to the continuum we spoke of above, I quote St. Augustine: "We move spiritually not by our feet, but by our desires." As the desire for union with God manifests itself both in daily life and in prayer, at some point we have reduced our activity to what is called simplified affective prayer, that is, to a word, a couple of words, a gesture, or a generalized image — not a visualization — that involves the spiritual sense of sight. We may come to a point in the use of the sacred word (which is simply a gesture of our intention, hence an expression of love) when it drops out of consciousness, and we are more or less aware of a general sense of peace, or of being grasped by God, or of just being restful and quiet. What has happened is that the intentionality renewed again and again by returning to the sacred word has become a habit and repeats itself. When the sacred word drops away, we enter into a no-man's/no woman's land in which the action of the Spirit meets the very simplified activity of renewing our intention by means of the sacred symbol. Then we have contemplation in the strict sense of the word. Until then, the Centering Prayer practice is really "acquired contemplation," a discipline of not dialoguing with the mind, or if the mind keeps thinking, of paying no attention to it. If the attraction of the dialogue becomes absorbing, we return to the sacred word to renew the purity of our original intention, which was to spend this time of prayer with God and to open and surrender to God.

In Centering Prayer, then, purity of intention is the primary focus of the practice. It is a matter of love. That is why it moves us away from our former dependence (conscious or unconscious) on thinking about God and on making acts of devotion to feel that we are doing something when we pray. The Spirit now has taken over our activity and prays in us. Our will is mingled with God's will in some mysterious way so that we have a sense of well-being or a conviction of being with God or in God. Sometimes sensible consolation overflows into the body, but it is not required for the fruits of this prayer. Centering Prayer becomes contemplation when the work of the Spirit absorbs our prayer and takes over. This can eventually be our habitual state of prayer, which is resting in God. We did not get to that state, of course, by our own efforts.

But let us return to the original objection based on the tradition that says, "Well, you folks may have a good method of contemplation, but the tradition has consistently warned that we should not start out at that point. What do you say to that?"

That is a significant objection. We are being accused of starting the cure for bad Lectio Divina before we have incurred the disease. I am convinced that one can begin Lectio at any one of the four stages — reading, reflecting, responding, or resting. In fact, some are better off beginning with resting in God precisely because of our cultural conditioning. Lectio is a dynamic process; that's why we emphasize its nature as relationship. The relationship quality of Centering Prayer implies all four levels. If one does not have the first three stages of Lectio worked into one's psyche, Centering Prayer will gently attract the practitioner to go back and fill in the space. Centering Prayer will lead one back to the earlier stages of Lectio because they are an integral part of the whole organic process. We will want to know how we got where we are. This is not just theory.

The Contemplative Outreach network contains many witnesses to this statement's practical validity. From an initial access point in Centering Prayer, these people have been moved to a fuller engagement with the whole Christian contemplative and scriptural tradition.

Centering Prayer fits well into the tradition of Lectio. But it fits in at a special place and serves a special purpose. One bishop told me that all his other devotional practices were enhanced when he began practicing Centering Prayer every day. For the first time he understood why he was doing them and how they fit into the organic development of his spiritual life. In fact, Centering Prayer *is* Lectio in the broad sense of the word. We are just beginning at a place that has not normally been recommended up until now, but we are doing so for good reasons and are getting good results. The tradition of Lectio Divina has always taught that we can go from one level to another even in the same period of prayer. Every one of the stages is enhanced if we have accessed the final one. If we could persuade people to start Centering Prayer, especially intellectuals who are not likely to experience contemplation without first disciplining their compulsion to reflect, all of the things that they do will become better. Their daily prayer will be more interactive, their reflections will have the unction of the Holy Spirit, and their conversation will touch other people's hearts much more than before. We are talking here about love. This is also what distinguishes Centering Prayer from Eastern methods. Eastern methods are primarily concerned with awareness. Centering Prayer is concerned with divine love.

The late Fr. Dan O'Hanlon, a distinguished Jesuit and authority in interreligious dialogue, writes, "I made the discovery, through contact with Asian practice, that one can move toward the goal of prayer beyond words and concepts without necessarily beginning with words and concepts." That, I think, is a challenge and an insight from the East that we should seriously take to heart.

The Eastern traditions put greater emphasis on what the self can do and hence contain the innate hazard of identifying the true self with God. The Christian tradition, on the other hand, recognizes God present but distinct from the true self. In other words, our uniqueness remains and becomes the vehicle for the divine expression, which was why we were created: to share by grace in the oneness of the Father and the Son.

Centering Prayer comes out of the Christian tradition and supports all the traditional devotions by illuminating their source. Thus it becomes the foundation for a much more fruitful apostolate and of relationships that are truly unselfish with other people, the cosmos, the earth, ourselves, and the Trinity. In other words, Centering Prayer is the Trinity living the divine life within us. It is eminently a Trinitarian prayer and implies the Incarnation, the Divine Indwelling, the Mystical Body of Christ, the Seven Gifts of the Spirit — the great dogmatic teachings that are generally regarded by theologians as the most important principles relating to the spiritual journey.

In teaching Centering Prayer, we do not normally say much about these principles at first because the introductory workshops and initial follow-up are not a theological course. Later on, however, we need to show how Centering Prayer, under other names and forms, has been expressed in the tradition. "How-to" methods have been clearly delineated in earlier ages. Centering Prayer is a re-expression, in a form adapted to our time, of the apophatic tradition that was initially developed by the Desert Fathers and reported by Cassian, but has its roots much earlier. It is already adumbrated in St. Paul. What the Desert Fathers did was to practice continuous prayer long enough to realize that to persevere required a method. One method they followed to get to the inner chamber was the repetition of a particular scriptural verse such as "O God, come to my assistance." This is described by Cassian in Conference Ten and corresponds to the practice we call in Contemplative

Outreach the Active Prayer Sentence. This is basically a practice to stay in direct contact with God in every activity all day long (see my *Invitation to Love*, p. 133, and *Open Mind, Open Heart*, p. 133).

Another practice, one that comes even closer to the method of Centering Prayer, is described by Abba Isaac in Cassian's Ninth Conference. "We need to be especially careful," Abba Isaac begins: "The gospel precept instructs us to go into our room and to shut the door so that we may pray to our Father." Liturgists may have a hard time with that text, but it might be a consolation to them to reflect that in light of the doctrine of the Communion of Saints and the Mystical Body, whether one is alone or with others, every genuine prayer is liturgy. "We pray in our rooms," continues the Abba, "when we withdraw our hearts completely from the tumult and noise of our thoughts and worries and secretly and intimately offer our prayer to the Lord. We pray with the door shut when, without opening our mouths and in perfect silence, we offer our petitions to the one who pays no attention to words but who looks hard at our hearts." This fourth-century Desert Father's teaching foreshadows the magna carta of the apophatic tradition that is found in chapter 5 of the *Mystical Theology* of the sixth-century Syrian monk Denis known for centuries as St. Dionysius the Areopagite and more recently as Pseudo-Dionysius.

The original monks intuited that a structured lifestyle was not enough for growth in prayer. There had to be added an interior practice. All through the Christian contemplative tradition we are reminded of the invitation of the gospel, "Go into your room and shut the door!"

Centering Prayer is heir to that school of prayer. It is based primarily on *The Cloud of Unknowing*, but I have incorporated elements in our presentation of Centering Prayer that resonate with other Christian spiritual classics. I have drawn from St. Francis DeSales and St. Jane de Chantal the idea of the gentleness with which to return to the sacred word. This emphasis is missing in the *Cloud*. I lean heavily on the teaching of St. John of the Cross in *The Living Flame of Love* (stanza 3, vv. 26–59), where he describes the transition from discursive meditation to contemplation.

Throughout the centuries the apophatic tradition has been treated with more or less discretion, sometimes going too far one way, sometimes too far in the opposite direction. We cannot undiscriminatingly trust any of the spiritual masters. Each is conditioned by his or her times and culture, at least in some degree. Looking at the tradition, we have to know how to read the Fathers and to bring them into critical relationship with later writers and with modern psychology, exercising a certain caution regarding the exhortations of writers who did not have that knowledge. Now that we have the knowledge, it has to be used. It is knowledge that most people in our day understand, but it must be taught in such a way as not to offer merely a self-help program.

If people go to the trouble of coming to an introductory workshop, they must have been inspired by something. Sometimes it is curiosity or the hope of finding a suitable group to pray or talk with. It seems to me that it may also be the Spirit at work. If people are not ready for the practice, they will just give it up when they go home. If they are ready, they will continue to walk the path and Contemplative Outreach will continue to grow. The charism is only ten years old; no organization can prove itself in that short a time. But at least we have witnessed some encouraging signs.

Contemplative Outreach as a network is primarily a process. This process listens to the needs of the people who are growing in contemplative experience and tries to respond appropriately to them as we continue our pilgrimage into the unknown.

Chapter 12

The Rosary as Contemplative Prayer

T HE ROSARY HAS BEEN WITH US NOW since the early Middle Ages. Its invention at that time was a stroke of genius because in those days there were no books, and when ordinary folks went to church on Sundays, they could not understand what the gospel was saying because it was proclaimed in Latin. Thus the common people did not have access to the Scripture. The rosary, based on repetition of the "Our Father," which Jesus gave us, and portions of the Scripture that make up the "Hail Mary," put these simple vocal prayers in a form that ordinary lay persons could easily recite. In effect, the rosary became the office of lay persons. It also gradually became for some a method leading to contemplative prayer, although it obviously is a concentrative method as distinguished from the receptive one we are familiar with in Centering Prayer.

Tradition, as I understand it, has always maintained that there are three ways of saying the rosary. We can unite two or all three, if we want to. The basic prayer of the rosary is the recitation of the vocal prayers, that is, just saying the Paters ("Our Father") and Aves ("Hail Mary") as they are grouped on the beads — a Pater on the large bead, followed by ten Aves on the smaller ones. Each of these groupings — one Pater, ten Aves, and a concluding doxology — is known as a decade.

A significant advance in the development of the rosary devotion came when reflection on the great mysteries of the faith was added to the simple recitation of the vocal prayers. Each of the rosary's fifteen decades became associated with one of the great feasts of Jesus and Mary celebrated in the liturgy, such as the Annunciation, the Visitation, the Nativity, the Presentation, the loss of the boy Jesus in the temple — to cite the first five of the fifteen mysteries. (The term "mystery" refers to the grace of the event, the belief that God was somehow present in the particular event and uniquely revealed through it.) The rosary thus became a true compendium of the liturgy. Those reciting the fifteen decades of the rosary in the course of a day or a week were able to access whole areas of Scripture that would otherwise have been closed to them because of lack of education or a knowledge of the Latin language. This practice — the second way of saying the rosary — enabled people to deepen their faith by joining to the vocal prayers their own reflections on these great mysteries. The third way of saying the rosary was simply to rest in the presence of God, Mary, or one of the mysteries.

Suppose you practiced the recitation of a significant part of the rosary — say, five decades — as a daily devotion. Where would this lead you? Into a deepening friendship with Christ. In the moment you began to pray, you made an act of faith in God's presence and thus reconnected with the grace of your baptism. In baptism the divine Trinity, Father, Son, and Holy Spirit, enters into our inmost being and dwells there unless we deliberately oppose this presence by some very serious and fully deliberate sin.

At some point in our life we have to ratify what was done in baptism and make it our own; otherwise its full fruition will be limited. The only way to make something our own is to take responsibility for it. That implies reflection and choice. In any case, through baptism we become a cell in the Mystical Body of Christ. The same Spirit that dwells in Jesus, the living and glorified Christ, also dwells in us, so we become living members of the body of Christ extended in time. The Mystical Body of Christ manifests itself in the Christian community through the proclamation of the gospel, the Eucharistic prayer, but especially in

Holy Communion. Notice, the term is not "holy conversation," but "Holy Communion," which implies the intuitive sense of Christ's presence in which we do not have to say anything, but simply enjoy his presence as we consent to the truth and love that he imparts to us. Christ is always present within us in his divine nature as the Eternal Word of the Father. Holy Communion is meant to awaken us to the abiding presence of Christ begun in baptism, deepened in the sacrament of Confirmation, and deepened still more by our personal prayer and frequent reception of the Eucharist. Essential to Christianity is growth in relationship with Christ — a relationship that is constantly deepening and addressing itself to every level of our being. Not just our body, mind, or imagination, not just our heart, but our inmost being where the word resonates in silence and where divine union is effected. Once we have heard the word of God at that deep level, we have finally heard the full message of the gospel.

The rosary, it seems to me, is in the service of that project in much the same way as Lectio Divina, which we have already discussed at some length. The same principles are involved. The way we develop friendship with Christ is by means of reflecting on the mysteries of his life. The rosary is an organized way of helping people to reflect on the mysteries without having to read the whole of Scripture, which as we saw, was not available until relatively recently. In a very simple way, day after day, people would recite and reflect on the fifteen mysteries. Thus they would immerse themselves in a biblical environment and be empowered to relate daily life to these fundamental sources of Christian inspiration. As they went to work or performed their chores at home, they often carried a rosary with them and said maybe a decade from time to time, much as people today sometimes say the rosary commuting or waiting for a bus.

The rosary, of course, does not have to be said at one sitting. There is no obligation to say a certain number of decades at a time. But it makes good sense to have a specific time, if we are going to say the rosary as a principal devotion, so that we can give it our full attention. We can then use it as the basis for our conversation with Christ. A regular if not daily interview is the essential discipline of getting acquainted with anybody, including God.

Just as in Lectio Divina, there is an inherent movement from reflection to simply resting in God. Suppose you give a half hour to the rosary each day. Suppose as you are reflecting on the mysteries, you feel an inward attraction to be still in the presence of Our Lady and just absorb the sweetness of her presence with your inner spirit. You may sense the closeness of the divine presence within you as well as the closeness of Our Lady. This is what is meant by the term "resting in God." Moving beyond vocal prayers and beyond reflection when you feel the attraction to be still is the path to contemplation. This is the moment you should feel free to stop saying the vocal prayers and to follow the attraction to be still, because vocal prayers and discursive meditation are both designed to lead one gradually to that secret and sacred place. That is their whole purpose. Many people do not understand this and think that they have to complete a certain number of decades or a certain number of prayers. This is not the purpose of the rosary.

When you are communing with a friend or loved one, the conversation has to be spontaneous, and when inclined to rest in each other's presence, you just remain quiet. When the other person speaks or when you want to say something, it breaks that particular level of communicating and you go back to conversation. When the sense of resting in God passes, you can go back to your recitation of the rosary where you left off. If you do not have time to go back, it does not matter. There is no obligation to finish anything. Indeed, the compulsion to complete a certain number of vocal prayers hinders the spontaneity of contemplative prayer. Inner freedom is needed to follow the movement of the Spirit both in our reflections and in our relating to silent communication. This freedom is refreshing.

I know many people who have spontaneously learned to pray the rosary that way. But we must also teach people to pray it that way. Many come upon the attraction to be still in spite of themselves or by chance and feel guilty because they are not finishing the designated number of vocal prayers. The Spirit led them into that quiet space, but unwittingly they sometimes oppose the Spirit calling them into silence because of their preconceived ideas. In the old days one completed a certain number of decades to gain the indulgences. That practice has diminished now, and whatever its value it should never have been allowed to interfere with the movement of the Spirit leading us to contemplation. In that rest we hear the word of God at the deepest level, are assimilated to Jesus Christ, and begin to absorb what Paul calls the "mind of Christ" (1 Cor. 2:16), which might be summed up as the experience of the fruits of the Spirit and the Beatitudes. When the fruits of the Spirit are overflowing into our daily life, we experience the real fullness of the Christian life. Then prayer is constantly feeding into our daily activity. Our apostolate or ministry — and I include family life and parenting among the greatest ministries of Christian life — is going to become more effective. The whole purpose of the rosary is to lead to this deep experience of Our Lady, who together with Jesus breathes the Spirit into us. It is not so much the quantity of prayer that is important, but its quality. The development of faith and love is the fruit of reflecting on the mysteries of the rosary and especially of resting in them.

We had a lay brother at our monastery at Spencer, Massachusetts, who was a great lover of the rosary. When I entered in 1944 at Valley Falls, Rhode Island, before the fire that forced the community to move to Spencer, this dear brother, whose name was Brother Patrick, was in charge of milking the cows. His fingers and hands had gotten huge from hand milking over many years. He was permanently bent over from sitting underneath the cows day after day during milking time. He had great devotion to the rosary and was always saying it. In fact, he never stopped saying it. We have a picture of him during his last moments, and you can see his lips are parted, still reciting the prayers of the rosary. For him the rosary had become a kind of scaffolding that enabled him to occupy his hands with a very simple kind of activity so that his body did not interfere with his constant prayer. Inside the scaffolding was the real edifice: his interior devotion to Our Lady and his contemplative union with God. For those for whom the beads have become a scaffolding for their union with God, their contemplation is not hindered by saying the beads all the time, even in the midst of activity. On the contrary, this continuous repetition seems to sustain their deep interior prayer. Most people, however, until they come to such a state of prayer, find that in order to enter fully into the deep rest that the Spirit is infusing, they need to be free of any other activity. Otherwise the repetition becomes mechanical.

Brother Patrick was famous for saying the beads nonstop. He carried them everywhere. We used to sleep in cubicles in a common dormitory on boards that were hung on two-by-fours on each end of the cell. The straw mattress that was laid on top of the boards was even harder than the boards. One night when everyone was asleep, there was a terrible crash. The boards on which Brother Patrick's straw mattress lay had fallen to the cement floor. Everybody jumped up in bed. There were a few moments of dead silence. The next thing we heard was "Hail Mary, full of grace...."

On every occasion that prayer was Brother Patrick's first response. Later in life when he got so old he could not work anymore, he was living in the infirmary. He became quite deaf, so in order to help himself remember to say all the words of the rosary, he got into the habit of repeating them.

He loved to repeat them out loud when he did not think anyone was around, but he could not hear himself. So he would say, "Hail Mary, full of grace... full of grace... full of grace; the Lord is with you... with you... with you." One day a novice was in the infirmary cleaning the chapel and Brother Patrick was there saying his rosary out loud as usual. Brother Patrick came to the place, "Blessed are you among women." And then, as was his custom, he kept repeating the last word, "Women... women... women...." The novice was shocked and rushed out to find the abbot. "That old monk in the infirmary must be having terrible temptations!" he blurted out. "All he can think about is women!"

In March 1950, the monastery in Valley Falls, Rhode Island, burned down. There is a picture of Brother Patrick sitting there watching the blaze. His beads are in his hand.

There are many people who have understood the great power of the rosary and have been taught how to say it through the grace of the Spirit. It has become for them not just continuous prayer, but continuous contemplative prayer. As they say it, they are frequently resting in the mystery of the divine presence beyond the other mysteries, and they are resting at such a deep level that even the activity of fingering the beads and moving their lips does not interfere with their rest. They do not have to stop doing what they are doing because God is so present in their hearts that their every movement is a prayer. I think that is the way Our Lady prayed. For her to think about praying or to try to do so could have been a distraction because she was prayer in her very being. She *was* prayer. Her relationship with God, which is the essence of prayer, was so close that whatever she did was prayer without her thinking about it.

The rosary is definitely a means to contemplative prayer. That is why Our Lady in various apparitions in the last one or two hundred years keeps saying, "Please say the rosary." Maybe this is just my prejudice as a contemplative, but in my view what she means is not only to pray, but to pray in such a way as to become a contemplative. In other words, "Say the rosary in a contemplative way." Thus it is contemplative prayer that she is primarily requesting. As the regular recitation of the rosary deepens our understanding of the mysteries and nudges us beyond the mysteries into periods of contemplative prayer, different levels of union with the divine presence open up within us. Centering Prayer is simply another way of moving in the same direction. It might also be useful to those who say the rosary to give them some taste of contemplative prayer, so that they could more easily recognize the call of the Spirit to interior silence when they are reciting the Our Fathers and Hail Marys. Moments of contemplative prayer bring about deep rest and deep bonding with God. As a consequence of this bonding, we have the courage and trust to face our mixed motivation and the dark side of our personality. The purification of our mixed motivation and selfishness can now begin because we can acknowledge our deepest wounds only to someone whom we know loves us and whom we trust. Love is the only way a human being can come into full being. If this has been withheld in a significant degree, then we have developed coping mechanisms and are driven to seek happiness in pleasure, affection, and esteem symbols that are fantastic, and hence their inevitable frustration gets us tied up into emotional knots.

In moments of contemplation and as its ripe fruit, God shows us gently, little by little, what needs to be changed in us. This is why contemplative rest when it is part of the rosary completes it and fulfills its great promises. In the mysteries of the rosary, one sees how God purifies his servants. We realize, "This must be the way it is." We too can then lovingly submit to our own purification.

The principles I have emphasized for the proper use of the rosary apply to the other great devotions of the

Christian tradition: the Stations of the Cross (originally introduced by St. Francis of Assisi), the chanting of the psalms, the liturgical prayer called the Divine Office, adoration of the Blessed Sacrament, the veneration of icons, and especially Lectio Divina.

Chapter 13

The Charismatic Renewal and Contemplation

THE PENTECOSTAL MOVEMENT began to attract Catholics in the late 1960s. It developed rapidly, manifesting a number of the charisms and charismatic ministries that Paul was acquainted with in the early Church. The movement became known among Catholics as the Charismatic Renewal. The renewal speaks powerfully to two needs that Catholics experience today with special urgency: the need for prayer, or, more exactly, for the experience of prayer, and the need to feel part of a Christian community. Ordinary parish structures are supposed to provide for these basic needs. In recent times however, especially in areas where large congregations are the rule, these aspirations are not adequately fulfilled. The experience of community provided by charismatic prayer groups, with their lively personal concern for one another and spontaneous expressions of affection, has seemed like a breath of fresh air to many Catholics hungering for an integral Christian life. For such as these, the renewal has brought freedom from stereotyped forms of prayer and ritual, the support and encouragement of spiritual friendship, and a new understanding and love of the Christian community as the living manifestation of Christ.

In the numerous prayer groups that have sprung up as a result of the renewal, some manifest a fundamentalist orientation. Wherever the fundamentalist influence has been strong, there has been a tendency to place special emphasis on the charismatic gifts of the Spirit enumerated by St. Paul in 1 Corinthians 12, especially the gift of tongues. In groups that have retained a predominantly Catholic influence, however, the desire for the knowledge and understanding of the Seven Gifts of the Holy Spirit has emerged. These are the gifts of wisdom, understanding, knowledge, counsel, piety, fortitude, and reverence. In addition, serious efforts have been made to provide a conceptual framework for the renewal based on traditional Catholic theology. These concerns have raised the question of the relationship of the renewal to the various forms of Christian spirituality of the past and, in particular, its relationship to contemplative prayer and the mystical life. To those in search of a sound program for continuing spiritual growth in the context of renewal, the contemplative tradition of the Church has important things to say.

In opening itself to the tradition, however, the renewal should remain true to its primary inspiration, which is listening to the Spirit as she strengthens, consoles, and guides us with her unfailing inspirations. Thanks to the renewal, the spontaneity of the early Christian communities described by Paul and the Acts of the Apostles, is being rediscovered in our time. The first believers in the incarnate Word of God gathered in communities around the risen Christ to listen to his word in Scripture, to celebrate its significance in the liturgy, and to be transformed into the Word made flesh by the Eucharist. The presence of the Spirit was palpably manifested in these assemblies by means of the charismatic gifts. The gift of tongues seems to have been given, along with faith in Jesus and the acceptance of baptism, to encourage the individual believer; hence, its use in public worship was regulated by Paul. Interpretation of tongues, prophecy, miracles, healing, discernment of spirits, words of wisdom, prophecy, inspired teaching, administration, and other gifts provided for the spiritual and material needs of the various Christian communities (see 1 Cor. 12:8–10). These gifts were normally subject to the discernment of each community either directly or through the ministry of the elders and presbyters.

The continuing work of the Spirit developing the teaching of the Church on contemplative prayer and the mystical life must now be integrated into this scriptural model revived by the Charismatic Renewal. Unfortunately, the presentation of this teaching in the last two or three centuries has not been a faithful representation of the wisdom of the great masters of Christian contemplation. A full-scale renewal of the Church's spiritual tradition has begun in earnest only since the Second Vatican Council. The ascetical teaching that most priests, monks, and nuns received in seminaries and novitiates was influenced in varying degrees by certain heresies that have plagued the Church throughout the centuries. Concurrently, the mystical teaching of the spiritual masters of the Church was almost completely ignored. As a result, the Church has been a spiritual desert for the past several centuries and unable to nourish her children with the solid food of contemplative prayer.

A significant indication of this can be found in the massive movement of Catholics toward Eastern religions during the past three decades in search of the contemplative dimension that was lacking in their own religious training and milieu. A new formulation of the principles of the spiritual journey for Christians is urgently needed today that will be faithful to the tradition but expressed in contemporary language and understanding. Such formulation should assiduously avoid the negative influences of the heresies of the past, especially Manichaeism (which infected the ascetical teaching of Augustine), Jansenism (which exercised a doleful effect in French and Irish seminaries from the seventeenth century into our own time), Cartesianism (the philosophy of Descartes, which exercised a predominant influence in forming the excessively dualistic assumptions of Western culture), and legalism (which retarded the march of the Church into the modern world). A new formulation should take thorough account of contemporary developments in theological and scriptural studies and of the insights of psychology and sociology, especially those that bear directly on human development and consequently on the spiritual life. In developing the method and conceptual background of Centering Prayer, I have attempted to address some of these urgent needs.

The Church has always been faced with the task of integrating the knowledge and experience of each successive age into its inherited body of doctrine and practice. Although this task is becoming more difficult because of the proliferation of new sciences and the information explosion, the Church cannot avoid this responsibility. The ability to respond to the signs of the times in a prompt and inspired manner and the ability to absorb and integrate the genuine human values of every culture are charisms that the Church must cultivate if it is to appeal to the hearts and minds of the emerging global society. The Council of Jerusalem described in Acts 15 is a good example of these charisms at work. It should be noted that the Apostles were convinced of the direct inspiration of the Spirit in their decisions.

Let us turn now to the relationship between the spirituality of the Charismatic Renewal and the traditional teaching of the Church on contemplative prayer and the mystical life. The baptism of the Spirit seems to be the formal initiation by the Spirit into the charismatic experience. Some have received this grace without any apparent preparation. They have come in off the street, so to speak, and at the first prayer meeting found themselves confronted and, in many instances, confounded and overwhelmed by the presence of the Spirit or the person of Jesus. Such experiences remind one of the instant conversions related in Acts. Baptism of the Spirit evidently brings about dramatic changes in one's previous relationship to Jesus and the Spirit. While particular conversions differ widely, many reports describe the experience in such terms as these: a strong impression of being loved by God; the assurance of the total forgiveness of one's sins; a new awareness of Jesus as a real person instead of an abstract figure in ancient history; an ease in practicing virtue; a greater love and understanding of the Word of God in Scripture and liturgy; the ardent desire to praise God; an eagerness to bear witness to Jesus Christ as Lord and Savior. These and similar effects clearly indicate the special action of the Holy Spirit, which, in terms of traditional Christian spirituality, may be a sign of mystical grace.

There are, of course, also gradual ways of coming to these excellent dispositions. Similar effects have been observed in the course of good novitiates in religious communities, after sincere conversions, and during extended periods of intensive religious discipline. The essential sign of conversion, whether it comes instantly through baptism in the Spirit or more gradually through the practice of virtue, is that it provides a profound intuition into the goal to be pursued by Christian practice. It is a thrust in the fundamental direction that one's life should take as a follower of Christ. While baptism in the Spirit does not establish an advanced state of spiritual development, it is a manifest call to contemplative prayer. If the gift of tongues accompanies baptism in the Spirit, a further thrust in the direction of contemplative prayer is added. While those possessing the gift of tongues are able to exercise it at will, they do not understand the meaning of the words they are saying. They are simply aware that they are praying or praising God. Such a simple and loving attention to God is itself a beginning of contemplative prayer.

The contemplative tradition of the Church teaches that contemplative prayer is the normal development of the practice of the Christian life. The exercise of the gift of tongues as well as the reflective reading of the word of God in Scripture normally leads to a growing attraction for interior silence and prayer. Prayer groups as well as individuals experience this evolution. The initial fervor flowing from baptism in the Spirit, just as the initial fervor following commitment to Christ through some similar conversion experience, tends to settle down and to turn into dryness in prayer and devotional practices. Difficulty in discursive meditation, boredom with spiritual exercises, and restlessness with one's private or group prayer begins to predominate. These signs are the usual introduction into the dark night of sense, of which St. John of the Cross gave a classic description in *The Dark Night of the Soul*.

At this critical turning point in the spiritual journey, the traditional teaching of the Church about purification from the roots of sin is essential for members of prayer groups. Otherwise, they may give up praying altogether. They must be encouraged to see this period of pervasive dryness as a necessary stage in the growth of the risen life of Christ within them. In the model developed in Centering Prayer, these periods of dryness are explained as part of the purification of the unconscious, without which our initial experience of conversion suffers the same fate as the seed that falls on rocky ground described by Jesus in the parable of the sower. Another way of envisioning these times of dryness is as a more intimate sharing in the Paschal mystery. The emptying of Christ described by Paul in Philippians 2:5–10 has entered into them, like the leaven hidden in the dough described by Jesus in another of his parables. As humility grows, so do compassion for others, submission to God, and the kind of confidence in God that leads to self-surrender.

At this crucial period in one's spiritual development, it is important to realize the sharp distinction between charismatic gifts such as tongues, prophecy, healing, etc., and the Seven Gifts of the Spirit. According to Paul, the charismatic gifts (with the exception of tongues) are designed for the building up of the local community. They do not necessarily indicate that those who possess them are either holy or becoming holy through their exercise. If one is attached to them, they are an obstacle to genuine spiritual growth. For those who have received one or more of these gifts, this is clearly part of God's plan for their sanctification and a cause for gratitude. But they must learn to exercise these gifts with detachment and not take pride in themselves because they happen to be the recipients of a special grace. Generally God provides sufficient external trials to take care of this human tendency. Prophets, healers, and administrators can greatly benefit from opposition, because it tends to free them from the fascination of their gifts and to keep them humble.

The Beatitudes are more profound expressions of the Spirit and grow, together with faith and the expansion of divine love, in the hearts of mature Christians. Through the transforming path of the Beatitudes, the Spirit replaces the hesitations of human reason (even when enlightened by faith) with the certitude of divine inspiration. Each of the fruits of the Spirit and the Beatitudes should be studied in depth as a means of understanding and cooperating with the movements of the Spirit, which alone lead to holiness.

Christian transformation takes place under the power of the theological virtues — faith, hope, and charity. The Seven Gifts of the Spirit raise these virtues to the divine mode of functioning. One sees, feels, discerns, and loves in the same way God sees, feels, discerns, and loves. Ultimately, divine love becomes the source of one's conscious life and activity. "I" or "me" is no longer the center of motivation. Christ manifests himself in and through one's transformed human nature.

Paul himself emphasizes the distinction between charismatic gifts that are given to build up the body of Christ and the substantial gift of divine love. According to him, one possessing the charismatic gifts is still nothing unless one also possesses divine love (see 1 Cor. 13:1–3). Hence, the basic thrust of charismatic prayer and the exercise of the charismatic gifts should be ordered to the growth of faith, hope, and charity. To remain faithful to the clear invitation to divine union extended by God through the grace of baptism of the Spirit, one must not be diverted by secondary manifestations of spiritual development. Moreover, there is need for discernment with even the most genuine charismatic gifts. It is the duty of the community or its representatives to discern these gifts and to determine whether they spring from grace or from the natural energies of the unconscious. Those who possess them should willingly submit to this discernment for the good of the community. Otherwise, the exercise of the gifts may be destructive of the common good rather than a means of building up the body of Christ.

Along with the charismatic gifts, which may be given to anyone without a corresponding level of personal spiritual development, so-called "mystical" phenomena, such as clairvoyance, locutions, visions, levitation, trance states, and many others, may accompany spiritual development as one accesses the divine emerging from the ontological unconscious. These also are of little significance compared to the graces of interior transformation set in motion by the Seven Gifts of the Spirit. The unusual and sometimes showy character of "mystical" phenomena makes them a hazard for immature mystics. It is difficult for even advanced persons to avoid taking a certain self-satisfaction in them.

The Charismatic Renewal needs spiritual guides who are thoroughly qualified through knowledge and personal experience of contemplative prayer to distinguish what is essential from what is accidental in the spiritual path. They should be able to recognize when someone is being called by God to interior silence and solitude and when someone is being called out of solitude into some particular ministry or service. People must be encouraged to follow the attraction to interior silence in prayer even if this means not attending prayer meetings for a time. This is especially necessary if, because of the duties of one's state in life, one cannot attend prayer meetings and still have time to practice contemplative prayer. Periods of silence in the liturgy and during prayer meetings are essential for groups whose members are growing in prayer. To allow one another space in which to develop the contemplative dimension of the gospel is an integral part of commitment to a Christian community.

One of the most significant contributions to the renewal of the spirituality of the contemporary Church is an enthusiasm for Scripture. Scripture reading is the best place to construct a bridge between the renewal and the ancient tradition of contemplative prayer. The word of God is the source of Christian contemplation. Listening to that word at deepening levels of attention is the traditional method of apprenticeship to contemplative prayer. In the classic monastic practice of Lectio Divina, the reading of Scripture in an attitude of attentive docility led to the deep penetration of the sacred text, moving the hearts of believers to respond in spontaneous prayer. As regular practice transformed attention into intention, the love of God tended to supplant the flow of reflections and particular acts of devotion with the simplicity of resting in God. The movement from sacred reading to resting in God is part of the dynamics of a deepening life of prayer.

To develop the contemplative dimension of the gospel, charismatics have only to deepen their listening to the word of God in Scripture, remembering that this word also dwells within them. There is no opposition between the outward and inward word of God. They mutually confirm and reinforce each other. The inward word speaks in silence, in the directness of love. The word expressed in the proclamation of the gospel or in private reading of the sacred text is the same word that emerges from the eternal silence of the Father and is present in our inmost being, where he awakens our understanding to the divine mysteries to which Scripture points. We do not reject thinking, but go beyond thinking when attracted by the absorbing presence of the Spirit.

What is necessary is to be detached from concepts in relating to God, for Scripture reveals God as incomprehensible, infinite, and ineffable: "To what have you compared me?" (Is. 40:18) Commenting on these prophetic words of Isaiah, St. John of the Cross warns that if we have excessive reliance on concepts to go to God, we are likely to fall into human projections and the kind of image-making that God condemned with such force in the Old Testament. We must accept God as God is. Faith purified from attachment to any concept and love purified from attachment to consolation, even the most spiritual, knows God in the immediacy of divine union. Contemplative prayer is the best apprenticeship for divine union. It is the exercise of pure faith, trust, and love, proved by waiting for God without giving up or going away. It is letting go of the false self, the "old man" in Paul's terms, and the building of the "new man" — and the "new woman" — under the motivating power of the indwelling Spirit.

The risen Christ addresses us from without in order to teach us to listen inwardly to his spiritual impressions. The contemplative life is to live not only *in* God's presence but *out* of God's presence. We become the word of God through the transformation effected by faith, hope, and divine love. Then we will be witnesses to Christ in our very being.

Chapter 14

Toward Intimacy with God

In the second chapter I looked briefly at the three theological principles on which Centering Prayer is based: its *source* is Trinitarian, its *focus* is Christological, and its effects are *ecclesial*, that is, it bonds us with everyone else in the Mystical Body of Christ and indeed with the whole human family. In this chapter I would like to return to these principles in more detail, to see how they move from theology into the deepening experience of God's presence and action in our lives. The spiritual journey is our movement into this transcendent reality and the gradual assimilation of it over the course of a lifetime.

The source of Centering Prayer is the Trinity, God's life within us, begun in baptism or whenever we entered into the state of grace. The doctrine of the Divine Indwelling of the Most Holy Trinity is the most important of all the principles of the spiritual life. It means that *God's own life* is being communicated to us, but beyond the level of our ordinary faculties because of what might be called, to use a modern scientific analogy, its high frequency. It is so high in fact, that only pure faith can access the divine presence in its full actuality.

The doctrine of the Trinity affirms three relationships in the one God, whom tradition calls the Father, the Son (the Eternal Word of the Father), and the Holy Spirit. This is the principal mystery of the Christian faith.

"Father" in this context, encompasses every human relationship that is beautiful, good, and true, but it especially evokes the sense of parenting, of "sourcing." The doctrine of the Trinity has been developed in many different theological models over the centuries. Drawing on these models, we can affirm that the Father is the ground of all potentiality. The actualization of that potentiality within the Trinity is the Word. The Word is the Father coming to full expression of all that the Father is. In a sense the Father is nothing until he speaks the Word. He knows who he is only in the Son, only in his interior Word. The Spirit is the common bond of love that flows between the Father and the Son in total self-giving love. In other words, the emptying of the Father — the actualization of all that is contained in infinite potentiality — is expressed totally in the Eternal Word expressed within the Trinity. The Father pours himself into the Son. One might almost say that there is nothing left of Him. The traditional theological doctrine of circumincession teaches that the Father lives in the Son, not in himself. The Son in turn, in confronting this immense goodness that has been handed over completely and freely to him, gives himself back to the Father in a kind of embrace, or what certain Fathers of the Church have called "the most sweet kiss" of the Father and the Son. The Spirit, then, is the love of the Father and the Son, their common heart, so to speak. In the Trinity, there is no self. Everything is self-surrender. Everything is gift. Everything is love. Hence St. John the Evangelist affirms unconditionally, "God is love."

With the same movement that the Father manifests himself in the Eternal Word, all creation comes into being in and through the Word. Thus the Word is the creative source of everything that exists (see the Prologue of St. John's Gospel), expressing itself in different ways throughout the different levels of creation. Creation consists of various manifestations of infinite reality without in any way exhausting that reality.

The emptying of the Word in becoming incarnate is the visible expression of what the Father is doing all the time in expressing his interior Word. When that manifestation takes place in creation, it has to be expressed by some form of emptying. Divine love, when it enters creation, has to be crucified because there is no way in which that love can be fully expressed in created terms without the Father in some sense dying. In creating, God in some way ceases to be God. At least, God ceases to be God in the way he was before creation. God must become totally involved in creation because each creature expresses something of the beauty, the goodness, and the truth of the Eternal Word who is the absolute fullness of God's expression. Jesus Christ is the fullest manifestation of this extraordinary love that we call unconditional or divine love. This is the heart of the Christian mystery — mystery, not in the sense of an intellectual puzzle, but in the sense of wonder and awe, communicating a delight that is inexpressible and that demands as the only adequate response our total surrender. The Trinitarian relationships, of their very nature, invite us into the stream of divine love that is unconditional and totally self-surrendered. This boundless love emerges from the Father into the Son, and through the Son is communicated to all creation. The invitation is given to every human being to enter into the stream of divine love, or at least to venture a big toe into the river of eternal life. As we let go of our false self, we move into this stream of love that is always flowing and bestowing endless gifts of grace. The more we receive, the more we can give. And as we give, we open the space to receive still more.

When that immense project is translated into creation and, specifically, into human life, we run into difficulties because we arrive at full reflective self-consciousness without the intimate experience of God's presence and unconditional love. That is one of the points I have emphasized in the Spiritual Journey video tapes and in the book *Invitation to Love:* we come to full reflective self-consciousness without the experience of intimacy with God and without consciously sharing in the divine life. When we sit in contemplative prayer letting go of our usual flow of thoughts and feelings, which reinforce our false selves, then our hearts are opened by our intentionality to the divine Spirit who is already present. Thus we begin to find out who God is. The divine life is in fact going on within us twenty-four hours a day. Unfortunately we have habits of refusal and opposition that make this access extremely difficult without a disciplined and regular practice of prayer.

The source of Centering Prayer, then, is not some aspiration, expectation, or far off ideal, but rather its source is the transcendent reality of the divine life present within us right now in the measure of our faith. This marvelous gift is given in baptism and even in the desire for God. The latter, I venture to say, applies to many people who do not name God in the same way that Christians do, but who have the desire to enter into union with the Ultimate Reality.

When we are sitting in Centering Prayer, we may seem to be doing nothing, but we are doing perhaps the most important of all functions, which is to become who we are, the unique manifestation of the Word of God that the Spirit designed us to be.

The Trinitarian life is not a strategy, a program, or some kind of box into which we fit. It is rather an activity of grace that enables us to experience ever increasing interior freedom, even to the point that St. Augustine describes, "One has the freedom not to sin," that is, not to function out of the false self in any way at all. This is the freedom of the children of God.

The source of Centering Prayer is the Trinitarian life. Thus in this prayer we are trying to touch base, so to speak, with a life that is objectively — that is, really — present within us and that we access through faith, hope, and divine love. The exercise of these three theological virtues is precisely the transforming dynamism used by the Spirit to awaken in us the deeper levels of divine awareness. Paul says that "faith is the assurance of things hoped for" (Heb. 11:1). It is the invincible conviction that we are united to God before we can feel it or know it in any other way except through self-surrender. This is what opens the heart to what Paul calls the inpouring of divine love. "Hope does not disappoint us, because God's love has been poured into our hearts through the Holy Spirit that has been given to us" (Rom. 5:5). Thus the source of Centering Prayer, as a preparation for the contemplative life, is the Trinitarian life itself, which is going on inside us and is manifested by our desire for God, to seek the truth, and to pray.

The focus of Centering Prayer is Christological. The attraction of grace may have many different forms and aspects, but in the context of the Christian life it is focused on Jesus Christ. This means that as we sit in faith, opening to the fullness of the presence of God within us, we share the dynamic of the Paschal mystery. In other words, when we stop acting out of our false self and the emotional programs for happiness by deliberately entering into silence and solitude during the time of Centering Prayer, we are immersing ourselves in a special way in the Paschal mystery. The Paschal mystery is Christ's passion, death, and resurrection, the most comprehensive manifestation of who God is, as far as this can be expressed in human terms. The emptying of Jesus is the visible symbol or sign — indeed the actualization in creation — of the infinite emptying of the Ultimate Reality — Infinite Goodness throwing itself away in love.

In the midst of a community praying together in Centering Prayer is the Risen Christ. He is not visible to our eyes, imagination, or senses, but on the spiritual level we intuit the presence of the divine when it is strongly present, as we sometimes do in a sacred shrine and, at times, in our own hearts. The deep conviction of presence beyond words or thoughts that awakens the desire for God *is* the divine life going on within us, letting a spark of insight or bliss drop into our starving faculties to awaken the fire of divine love when it seems to be going out.

We are living in a world that rejects love and that affirms selfishness as the ultimate value. The pressure from society is constantly insinuating itself through our upbringing, education, and culture. Society as a whole is saturated with the non-God.

First we have to affirm our interior freedom to be who we are or who we want to be in the face of all worldly enticements, including the worldly enticements associated with the spiritual journey. We bring the false self with us into the spiritual journey and into our relationship with God. Perhaps for many years our relationship with God might be termed co-dependent because we deal with God in the magical way that is characteristic of children. An important fruit of contemplative prayer is to be purified of our childish ideas about God. As our idea of God expands, there is no word, no way, no gesture, that can articulate it anymore. Hence we fall into silence, the place we should have been in the first place.

God's first language is silence. There is no word in the Trinity except the Eternal Word, and that one Word contains everything. As St. John of the Cross writes: "It was said once, and said in absolute silence. And it is only in silence that we hear it."

We have to climb up to this kind of silence. This language is not taught in the Berlitz repertoire. We have to teach ourselves. The primary teaching of Centering Prayer is basically very simple and can be expressed in two words: "Do it!" It will then do you. But it requires doing it every day. That is extremely important when we consider the other influences that are bearing down upon us. At times in our lives we have to make choices and set up priorities. Once we are dealing with Christ as the primary focus of our prayer, there is no longer a question of simply choosing between good and evil. There is a question of choosing between good, better, and best. The exercises or methods that we used in the beginning may have to be set aside for better tools, and finally for the best tools when we have moved as far as our human faculties can move us with the help of grace. Then without doing anything, silence does everything in us.

There is another important aspect to the fact of Christ as the focus of Centering Prayer. Our intention in sitting down is to open to the presence of Christ, remembering that the passion, death, and resurrection of Jesus reveal the mystery of the Trinity more than any other event. We are assimilating the presence of Christ in Centering Prayer, regardless of what we feel and of what thoughts go by, as long as our intention is to identify with that presence.

Christ's passion, as I understand it, is our own human misery. He has taken upon himself all the consequences of the human condition, the chief of which is the feeling of alienation from God. That is the emotion he felt most poignantly on the cross when he cried out, "My God, my God, why have you forsaken me?" It is also at the heart of our own experience of the purification of the unconscious. The false self is invited to dissolve through the gradual process in which we come to know the dark side of our personality and our incredible possibilities for evil. But to experience this in the context of a loving God, in the context of being fathered and mothered by the divine life going on within us, is precisely what enables us to face that dark side and our capacity for evil without being blown away.

The metaphor of the spiral staircase that we developed in Chapter 8 emphasizes that as we go down in humility we experience a corresponding level of inner resurrection. The fullness of divine life of course is not permanently established until we come to the bottom of the pile of our emotional junk. The undigested emotional material of a lifetime has to be processed by the Divine Therapist before we can access the fullness of liberation from the false self. As Jesus said, "No one comes to the Father except through me," that is, without accepting what he has accepted. He has entered into and accepted the human condition just as it is for our salvation.

Redemption, in this light, is not a cloak over our sins, but the inner transformation of our attitudes and motivation into the mind and heart of Christ. This process secretly goes on during periods of Centering Prayer. One is sitting, so to speak, on the cross with Christ, identifying with him and relinquishing the obstacles in us that hinder the free flow of divine love.

Normally the signs of resurrection are experienced more in daily life than during prayer itself. Our best criteria for judging whether our faith experience is really bearing fruit is in the growth of our desire for God — not a particular desire for this or that experience, but a general loving hunger for God. This is the most certain sign that the divine life is becoming healthy, strong, and powerful within us.

When we are doing Centering Prayer in a group, we access the contact that each of us has already made with the divine presence within us. This is our special gift to the group. The presence of Christ becomes more powerful because of our respective contributions to the interior silence of the assembled community. The intensity of that reservoir of interior silence enriches everybody at a deeper level than they might be able to reach alone.

The third theological principle on which Centering Prayer is based is that Centering Prayer is ecclesial in its effects — ecclesial in the sense of the original meaning of the word, which indicates a social dimension, function, or reality. Once we begin the spiritual journey, there is no longer merely private prayer. Our prayer becomes a participation in the groanings of the Spirit for all the intentions and needs of the human family. This does not mean that we do not pray for our loved ones at other times. But it does mean that during the periods of Centering Prayer we enter into a sense of oneness with everyone else who is experiencing grace, and with the whole human family. At times we may actually feel this bonding. This bonding is the heart and soul of a Christian community. Without it one wonders how effective a gathering of Christians really is. Gathered to participate intentionally in the Paschal mystery, the Centering Prayer meeting becomes a liturgy without words, a celebration of each one's union with Christ and of our gratitude for participating in the inner life of the Trinity. Every little drop of that experience is of almost inconceivable value and vastly transcends the assembled community itself. In other words, the divine energy that is accessed by each one's participation in Christ's passion, death, and resurrection becomes a kind of universal prayer for the needs of the whole human family. It has a radiation that is truly apostolic, apostolic in the sense of transmitting the grace of Christ into this world.

It also means that our personal creative energies are being awakened. Most of us are probably not using our full potential precisely because we have been sitting on it. Once we have fully identified with the Paschal mystery and are willing to take the aches and pains of purification that are the way to inner resurrection, we may experience in various ways a further call to some kind of ministry. I hesitate to use the word "ministry" because the word is so hackneyed that people think in terms only of concrete activities that are well known. All I can say is that the ministries and the charisms that are announced by Paul in 1 Corinthians 12 are only examples of what the Spirit can do once we have identified with this process. Our prayer is certain to have an effect on others and to force us to express this love in daily life. We do not have to think about it too much because, when the time comes, we will know what we are supposed to do or it may happen spontaneously. It may also change several times in our lifetimes, especially if we begin this journey early enough.

The process of bonding throws light on what we mean by the doctrine of the Communion of Saints. The latter is not a club to which virtuous people belong after having paid their dues by way of asceticism, suffering, or austere penances. Still less is it something we access only by physical death. It is, rather, a participation in the divine life that is eternal and that has no past or future because it is entirely present. By becoming present to the present, we become present to everyone in the past and in the future and become their friend. Thereafter we are never alone. I recommend that when you pray alone you think of inviting relatives and friends who have passed on to come and join you. I don't know what precisely they are doing up there, but they are certainly interested in prayer and in you. The Communion of Saints includes not only those who are canonized, but also your old friends, parents, and ancestors. They are all together now in the love of God. Through contemplative prayer, we are moving into a realm of reality that influences the past and the future perhaps more than anything else we could do.

I would like to share with you an experience I had as a young man because something similar has repeated itself from time to time when I have been sitting in a group doing Centering Prayer, especially with those who are experienced in it and when the silence is deep. As a young college student, recent in my conversion (I had already made up my mind to enter the Trappist order over the strong opposition of my parents), I made a surreptitious trip to the monastery in Valley Falls, Rhode Island, to spend Easter there while pretending that I was staying on campus. Early Easter morning I was in the chapel of the guest quarters attending a private mass. As the celebrant raised the host, all of a sudden without knowing what happened, I was completely identified with Christ present in the host. That insight penetrated the whole of my being and lingered in various degrees of intensity for three days. During this time I hardly spoke to anyone because of the fear of losing the sharpness of that overwhelming grace. It left me with the kind of conviction for which you are willing to die rather than deny that it happened. That moment of absolute certitude, of course, was a special grace for a desperate young man trying to become a Trappist during World War II, when there was little hope of going anywhere except into the armed services.

If you take time to reflect, you may remember that there were certain moments of special grace in your life that orientated you with great power toward the Ultimate Mystery. Some people misinterpret such an experience as arriving at their final goal, or at least as something to hang on to for dear life. That is not the purpose of special graces. They are given in order to introduce us, by briefly lifting a corner of the veil, to the mystery that is actually going on all the time. That mystery is the fact that the Trinity is leading the divine life within us and that the consent of faith — like turning on the switch in a building that has been electrically wired — illumines our darkness with the divine light. Faith that the divine light is present within us — a conviction, not necessarily an experience — is the primary foundation of Centering Prayer.

In a Centering Prayer community we become one not just with the people in the room and all those truly seeking God; we also become one with everything that God has created: with nature, with art, with relationship with the service of others. This bonding effect gives us an inner desire to form community and to be faithful to it, even if with only one other person.

This bonding may lead in several directions. It gives us a sense of reverence for the tradition, for example, an eagerness to find out where Centering Prayer comes from. If I had started sharing the classics of the Fathers when I started teaching Centering Prayer, few would have paid much attention. We began with a practice that would reduce people's preconceived ideas about the tradition so that they would have a chance to see it from a new perspective. We used psychological paradigms because that is the language that seems most congenial in our time, at least for people in the West. Once the Centering Prayer practice had gotten established, then the effects of the bonding process began to appear. To some, it suggested a live-in community; to others, retreats of varying intensity to deepen their experience. It also suggested some kind of administrative apparatus designed to help people in their practice and to empower them to empower others. This led to a network or support system called Contemplative Outreach, which provides places and times for ordinary people leading ordinary lives to deepen their practice of contemplative prayer and this growth in the spiritual journey.

Bonding has the dimension of opening us to the possibility of sharing our spiritual experiences with others, not only for the sake of companionship but also for the sake of mutual encouragement. Private experience is not the last word on reality. It is an important factor; we need to follow our own inspirations, but we also need the prudence and humility to submit our experiences to others who are on the same path so that those of us who might be experiencing mere side effects of the process can be guided by those who are more mature in the journey. The contemplative community thus becomes a safeguard against exaggerations like experiences that go to people's heads or that are interpreted in childish ways. Without a lot of purification our ways of relating to God continue to be influenced by the false self. Bonding involves a willingness to let go of our own preferences and conveniences and to sacrifice them when circumstances or our primary duties require it.

This brings me to the final point: prayer cannot stand alone without action emerging from it. Contemplative prayer without action stagnates, and action without contemplative prayer leads to burn-out or running around in circles. Contemplative prayer sifts our contemplative vision and our ideas about what we should be doing. It enables us to blend the two and to bring the spirit of our contemplative commitment into daily life. The Trinity is always present within us. Our focus on God is not just for the time of prayer but for the whole day. The presence of God is going to accompany us into daily life whether in other forms of prayer, in our relationships, or in our workplace. Without trying to, but just by being in God as you go about your daily functions, you exercise a kind of apostolate. In your very joking you may be pouring grace into the atmosphere and into other people. All our activities need to come out of this center. Centering Prayer tends not only to access our spiritual nature, but to express the true self. We are coming from an inner freedom that more and more, without our thinking about it, expresses the mind of Christ in our particular daily lives through the welling up and flowing over of the fruits of the Spirit and the Beatitudes.

Thus, as we journey more deeply inward toward the source of Centering Prayer, which is the Trinitarian life within us, its effects lead us powerfully outward, toward the bonding that we call the Communion of Saints: the capacity to relate to one another with the unconditional love with which Christ relates to us.

Glossary of Terms

Apophatic/Kataphatic Contemplation: A misleading distinction suggesting opposition between the two. In fact a proper preparation of the faculties through kataphatic practice leads to apophatic contemplation, which in turn is sustained through appropriate kataphatic practices.

Apophatic: the exercise of pure faith; resting in God beyond concepts and particular acts, except to maintain a general loving attention to the divine presence.

Kataphatic: the exercise of the rational faculties enlightened by faith: the affective response to symbols, reflection, and the use of reason, imagination, and memory, in order to assimilate the truths of faith.

Attention: The focusing on a particular object such as the breath, an image, or a concept.

Awareness: The act of being aware of a particular or general perception; another term for consciousness.

Beatitudes (Matt. 5:1–10): A further development of the fruits of the Spirit.

Centering Prayer: A contemporary form of Prayer of the Heart, Prayer of Simplicity, Prayer of Faith, Prayer of Simple Regard; a method of reducing the obstacles to the gift of contemplative prayer and of facilitating the development of habits conducive to responding to the inspiration of the Spirit.

Consent: An act of the will expressing acceptance of someone, something, or some course of action; the manifestation of one's intention.

Consolations: Among spiritual writers, this term generally refers to the sensible pleasure derived from devotional practices such as Lectio Divina, discursive meditation, prayer, liturgy, and good works. Such consolations may arise from sensible stimuli, imagination, memory, and reflection, or from purely spiritual sources such as the fruits of the Spirit and the Beatitudes.

Contemplation: A synonym for contemplative prayer.

Contemplative Living: Activity in daily life prompted by the gifts of the Spirit; the fruit of a contemplative attitude.

Contemplative Prayer: The development of one's relationship with Christ to the point of communing beyond words, thoughts, and feelings; a process of moving from the simplified activity of waiting upon God to the ever increasing predominance of the gifts of the Spirit as the source of one's prayer.

Dark Night of Sense: Term coined by St. John of the Cross to describe a period of spiritual dryness and purification of one's motivation initiated by the Holy Spirit, hence also called passive purification.

Dark Night of Spirit: A purification of the unconscious beyond the Dark Night of Sense aimed at eliminating the last remnants of the false self.

Divine Energy: The presence and action of God throughout all creation.

Divine Therapy: A paradigm in which the spiritual journey is presented as a form of psychotherapy designed to heal the emotional wounds of early childhood and our mechanisms for coping with them.

Divine Union: Either a single experience of the union of all the faculties in God, or the permanent state of union called transforming union (see *Transformation*).

Ecstasy: The temporary suspension by the divine action of the thinking and feeling faculties, including at times the external senses, which facilitates the experience of the prayer of full union.

Emotional Programs for Happiness: The growth of the instinctual needs of security/survival, affection/esteem, and power/control, into centers of motivation around which our thoughts, feelings, and behavior gravitate.

False Self: The self developed in our own likeness rather than in the likeness of God; the self-image developed to cope with the emotional trauma of early childhood. It seeks happiness in satisfying the instinctual needs of survival/ security, affection/esteem, and power/control, and bases its self-worth on cultural or group identification.

Fruits of the Spirit (Gal. 5:22–23): Nine aspects of the "mind of Christ" manifesting the growth of the divine life in us: love, joy, peace, patience, kindness, generosity, faithfulness, gentleness, self-control.

Gifts of the Spirit:
   a. **Charismatic Gifts of the Spirit (1 Cor. 12:1–13)** are given primarily to encourage the Christian community, e.g., tongues, interpretation of tongues, prophecy, miracles, healing, discernment of spirits, words of wisdom, inspired teaching, administration.
   b. **Seven Gifts of the Spirit (Is. 11:2):** Habitual dispositions empowering us to perceive and follow the promptings of the Holy Spirit both in prayer and action: counsel, prudence, fortitude, reverence, wisdom, understanding, knowledge.

Human Condition: A way of describing the consequences of original sin, which are: illusion (not knowing how to find the happiness for which we are inherently programmed); concupiscence (the pursuit of happiness where it cannot be found); weakness of will (the inability, unaided by grace, to pursue happiness where it is to be found).

Intention: The choice of the will in regard to some goal or purpose.

Interior Silence: The quieting of the imagination, feelings, and rational faculties, in the process of recollection; the general, loving attentiveness to God in pure faith.

Intuitive Consciousness: The level of consciousness beyond rational thinking (not to be identified with bodily intuition), characterized by harmony, cooperation, forgiveness, negotiation to resolve differences, mutuality rather than competitiveness; a sense of oneness with others and of belonging to the universe.

Lectio Divina: Reading or, more exactly, listening to the book we believe to be divinely inspired; the most ancient method of developing the friendship of Christ, using Scripture texts as topics of conversation with Christ.

Method of Contemplative Prayer: Any prayer practice that spontaneously evolves or is deliberately designed to free the mind of excessive dependence on thinking to go to God.

    a. Practices spontaneously evolving toward contemplation: Lectio Divina, the Jesus Prayer, veneration of icons, the rosary, and most other traditional devotions of the Church rightly used.

    b. Practices deliberately designed to facilitate contemplation: 1. Concentrative: the Jesus Prayer, mantric practice (constant repetition of a word or phrase), Dom John Main's method of "Christian Meditation." **2. Receptive:** Centering Prayer, Prayer of Faith, Prayer of the Heart, Prayer of Simplicity, Prayer of Silence, Prayer of Simple Regard, Active Recollection, Acquired Contemplation.

Mystical Prayer: A synonym for contemplative prayer.

Original Sin: A way of explaining the universal experience of coming to full reflective self-consciousness without the inner conviction or experience of union with God.

Purification: An essential part of the process of contemplation through which the dark side of one's personality, mixed motivation, and the emotional pain of a lifetime, stored in the unconscious, are gradually evacuated; the necessary preparation for transforming union.

Spirituality: A life of faith in interior submission to God and pervading all one's motivation and behavior; a life of prayer and action prompted by the inspirations of the Holy Spirit; a disposition not limited to devotional practices, rituals, liturgy, or particular acts of piety or service to others, but rather the catalyst that integrates, unifies, and directs all one's activity.

Spiritual Attentiveness: The general loving attention to the presence of God in pure faith, characterized either by an undifferentiated sense of unity or by a more personal attention to one of the Divine Persons.

Spiritual Senses: A teaching common among the Fathers of the Church to describe the stages of contemplative prayer through the analogy of the external senses of smell, touch, and taste. The point of the comparison is the immediacy of the experience.

Thoughts: In the context of the specific method of Centering Prayer, an umbrella term for any perception at all, including sense perceptions, feelings, images, memories, reflections, commentaries, and particular spiritual perceptions.

Transformation (Transforming Union): The stable conviction of the abiding presence of God rather than a particular experience or set of experiences; a restructuring of consciousness in which the divine reality is perceived to be present in oneself and in all that is.

True Self: The image of God in which every human being is created; our participation in the divine life manifested in our uniqueness.

Typhonic Consciousness: According to contemporary anthropology, the level of consciousness characterized by development of a body-self distinct from other objects. It is characterized by the inability to distinguish the part from the whole, and to distinguish images in the imagination from external reality.

Ultimate Mystery/Ultimate Reality: The ground of infinite potentiality and actualization; a term emphasizing the divine transcendence.

Unitive Consciousness: The experience of transforming union together with the process of working this level divine love into all one's faculties and relationships.

Unloading the Unconscious: The spontaneous release of previously unconscious emotional material in the form of primitive feelings or a barrage of images or commentaries; it may occur both during the time of contemplative prayer and outside the time of prayer.

A Selected Bibliography

The Cloud of Unknowing. Ed. and intro. by William Johnston. New York: Doubleday & Co., 1973.

Hall, Thelma. *Too Deep for Words.* New York: Paulist Press, 1989.

Hauser, Richard, S.J. *In His Spirit.* New York: Paulist Press, 1982.

Keating, Thomas. *Open Mind, Open Heart.* Rockport, Mass.: Element Books, 1992.

———. *Invitation to Love: The Way of Christian Contemplation.* Rockport, Mass.: Element Books, 1992.

———. *The Mystery of Christ: The Liturgy as Christian Experience.* Rockport, Mass.: Element Books, 1992.

Mallory, Marilyn May. *Christian Mysticism Transcending Techniques.* Van Gorcum & Company (P.O. Box 43, Assen, The Netherlands).

May, Gerald. *Will and Spirit.* New York: HarperCollins Publishers, 1982.

———. *Addiction and Grace.* San Francisco: Harper & Row, 1988.

Merton, Thomas. *Contemplative Prayer.* New York: Doubleday & Co., 1971.

Higgins, John. *Thomas Merton on Prayer.* New York: Doubleday & Co., 1975.

John of the Cross, St. *The Dark Night.* In *The Collected Works of St. John of the Cross.* Trans. Kieran Kavanaugh, O.C.D., and Otilio Rodriguez, O.C.D. Washington, D.C.: ICS Publications, 1979.

Mulholland, Robert, Jr. *Shaped by the Word.* Nashville: Upper Room, 1985.

Nemick, Francis, and Marie T. Coombs. *Contemplation.* Wilmington, Del.: Michael Glazier, Inc., 1984.

Pennington, Basil. *Centering Prayer.* New York: Doubleday & Co., 1980.

Teresa of Avila, St. *The Interior Castle.* In *The Collected Works of St. Teresa of Avila.* Vol. 2. Trans. Kieran Kavanaugh, O.C.D., and Otilio Rodriguez, O.C.D. Washington, D.C.: ICS Publications, 1980.

Anthologies

McGinn, Bernard, ed. *The Foundations of Mysticism.* Vol. 1 of *The Presence of God: A History of Western Christian Mysticism.* New York: Crossroad, 1991.

Wiseman, James A., and Louis Dupré, eds. *Light from Light: An Anthology of Christian Mysticism.* New York: Paulist Press, 1988.

Farina, John, ed. *The Classics of Western Spirituality: A Library of the Great Spiritual Masters.* New York: Paulist Press. Multivolume set. See especially: John Cassian, *Conferences;* Gregory of Nyssa, *The Life of Moses;* Pseudo-Dionysius, *The Complete Works.*